# Quilt Designs from Decorative Floor Tiles

## Christine Porter

David & Charles

Christine has been a quilter for 15 years. She is a highly respected and experienced teacher who not only lectures and judges throughout Britain and the United States but who has also won awards for her quilts in both countries. Her special field of interest is translating floor-tile designs into quilts, and she particularly enjoys creating a contemporary look through her use of colour and fabric style.

Until recently, Christine was for many years co-editor of Britain's leading patchwork magazine, *Patchwork & Quilting*. In addition Christine is director of her own company, 'Cabot Quilting Conferences' which brings top international quilters to Britain to teach in luxury hotels, to share their skills with other quilters from around the world.

## *Dedication:*
### *To Daniel, Sam and Hannah, my adorable grandchildren.*

A DAVID & CHARLES BOOK

First published in the UK in 2003

Text and designs Copyright © Christine Porter 2003
Photography and layout Copyright © David & Charles 2003
Photography by Neil Porter

Distributed in North America
by F&W Publications, Inc.
4700 East Galbraith Road
Cincinnati, OH 45236
1-800-289-0963

A catalogue record for this book is available from the British Library.

ISBN 0 7153 1439 4 hardback
ISBN 0 7153 1444 0 paperback (USA only)

Printed in the UK by Butler & Tanner Ltd
for David & Charles
Brunel House    Newton Abbot    Devon

Executive Editor Cheryl Brown
Desk Editor Sandra Pruski
Executive Art Editor Ali Myer
Designer Lisa Forrester
Production Controller Ros Napper

Visit our website at www.davidandcharles.co.uk
David & Charles books are available from all good bookshops; alternatively you can contact our Orderline on (0)1626 334555 or write to us at FREEPOST EX2110, David & Charles Direct, Newton Abbot, TQ12 4ZZ (no stamp required UK mainland).

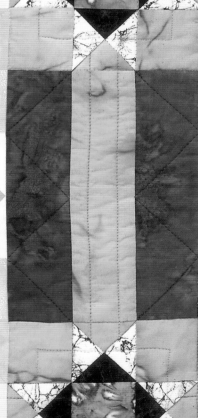

# Contents

# From the Beginning

The use of tiles to decorate buildings is as old as recorded history and examples can be found from all the major civilizations. The two strongest influences on the development of tiles in Northern Europe came from the Roman Empire and from Islam, and both can be clearly traced through from the Middle Ages to the present day.

In the 13th and 14th centuries, tiled floors were used in many of the great monastic buildings and fragments still exist. Beautiful tiles were also used in some of the great cathedrals. Spectacular examples in multicoloured mosaics can still be seen in Spain, France and especially Italy, in the cathedrals of Siena, Florence and in San Marco in Venice and elsewhere throughout Northern Europe. However, by the end of the 16th century decorative floor tiles had largely dropped out of fashion.

The unprecedented boom in building in the 19th century – both private houses and more importantly churches and public buildings, such as municipal offices, children's hospitals and railway stations – created a huge demand for decorative tiles. Production techniques were quickly developed to meet that demand. Tile-making factories sprang up in the English Midlands and by 1870 tiles were being used to decorate walls and floors in public buildings and houses, large and small, throughout Britain and what was then the British Empire.

One of those factories, at Ironbridge in Shropshire, has now been converted into the Jackfield Tile Museum and provides a fascinating storehouse of information. It was an important piece in the jigsaw that has become this book. It is clear that the Victorian tile manufacturers looked to great medieval examples of tiled floors for their inspiration. Arthur Maw, one of the pioneers of tile design and production, and at one time the largest tile producer in the world, took his sketchbooks (and his family) to Italy and elsewhere in Europe to sketch and copy tile designs there.

When we visited the Museum we were privileged to be able to look at Arthur Maw's original sketchbooks

and to admire the fine pen-and-wash illustrations that he brought back from his travels, including a spectacular and beautifully detailed rendition of the floor in San Marco in Venice.

In Maw's factory, and others like it owned by Minton and Wedgwood, those designs were reproduced as tiles and the variety of patterns that were on offer was astonishing. Catalogues issued at the time list and illustrate hundreds of tiles and patterns for whole floors, fireplaces and shop-door fronts and included a section on borders, all of which could be ordered in any number of combinations by architects and builders.

Looking at those catalogues, I was struck by how similar the designs were to traditional blocks that have been used throughout the ages in patchwork quilts. Another piece of the jigsaw fitted into place as I recalled how women from all over Europe had taken their traditional designs with them when they emigrated to America. These women incorporated the patterns into the quilts they so lovingly made under the hardships of frontier life and during the seemingly endless treks to settle in the West.

It was all there – the tile catalogues could easily have been traditional patchwork catalogues. I had no need to look further. The two traditions had run side by side.

**Above left**: 19th century drawing in progress
**Right**: Maw's catalogue designs
**Below and facing page**: Tiles that inspire

# From Tiles to Quilts

The inspiration for my quilts comes from the floors beneath my feet. I am fortunate enough to live in an historic city blessed with many medieval and Victorian churches. It was at the beginning of my adventure into patchwork that I discovered that the traditional block designs I was learning to sew were actually identical to the floor-tile patterns in several local churches.

I started to take my camera out with me to record the various designs, and as I did so I discovered more and more different patterns. Looking from books on traditional patchwork blocks to my photographs, I was able to identify parts of patterns and gradually ideas for quilts came to me. 'Ohio Star', 'Variable Star', 'Snowball', '54-40 or Fight', 'Square Within a Square' and many more designs were all there at my feet.

My initial colour palette was set for me by the tile designers, but I was also inspired by the fabrics I saw in quilt shops. So I set out on the journey that led to this book and the making of my floor-tile quilts. Alongside each quilt that represents a floor, I have created a further quilt based on the same blocks. By using contemporary fabrics I have been able to highlight how the use of colour and texture affects the design potential, an enjoyable process that has made collecting appropriate fabrics a real joy.

After visiting many churches, I began to look further afield and found floor tiles in unusual places – on garden paths, in conservatories, in hallways and porches. Hospitals, butchers shops and public buildings yielded yet more and I even found amazing tiles in Spanish hotel bathrooms.

The cathedral in my own city of Bristol has exquisite, highly coloured marble designs by the altar and along the nave. These were laid at the turn of the 19th century by a Mr Pearson, who also laid similar though less intricate designs in Truro Cathedral in Cornwall. The tile designs to the side of the altar reminded me of Chinese lanterns and I developed a diamond template so that I could make the floor quilt. Then I found that I could take that design one step further. (See pages 72–79.)

I could not resist the zigzag design running alongside the choir stalls (opposite, below left). This is a really traditional way of setting strippy quilts and I resolved to use it both in its original form and in a folksy look using mostly Roberta Horton's plaids and stripes. (See pages 88–95.)

Looking at a tile in detail can lead to a quilt that barely resembles it, but that fires the imagination. Peeking under a carpet in a 19th century building yielded special results as you can see from the splendid '54:40 or Fight' block found in the Clifton Club, Bristol (opposite, far right inset). By careful use of colour and by combining this block with another, I was able to create the illusion of a curve when in fact all the piecing is straight. (See pages 38–45.)

Simple designs can sometimes explain the old adage 'less is more' and I found the tiles of Bristol's St Stephen's Church gave me licence to develop the 'Square Within a Square' block, which has to be the easiest to make. The 'Flying Geese' border adds a fun element to the contemporary version of this quilt. (See pages 30–37.)

Sometimes tiles turn up in the most unexpected places and the chemist's shop in Ambleside in

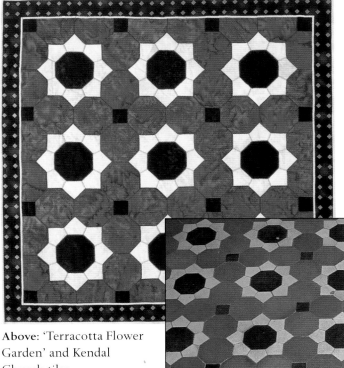

**Above:** 'Terracotta Flower Garden' and Kendal Church tiles

**Above:** 'Clifton Stars' and the tiles of the Clifton Club, Bristol

the Lake District is one such place. I had not seen this unusual cross design before, or its border, so I enjoyed the challenge of making both the replica and the contemporary version in its primary colours. (See pages 80–87.)

Visiting Kendal Church, also in the Lake District, I found a charming flower pattern on tiles by the font. I was able to exploit it using two completely different methods – English paper piecing and fusing fabric to a background. This is the beauty of tile designs; they act as a starting point from which to explore different techniques and colour combinations. (See above left and pages 54–63.)

The churches of Italy provide a paradise for floor-tile hunters and every possible combination of geometric

patterns is to be found, literally a feast for the eyes. More complex designs require completely different sewing techniques and my interpretation of part of the amazing tiled floor in St Mark's Cathedral in Venice presented a real piecing challenge. I have designed four small projects based on this large quilt. (See pages 96–104.)

Collecting fabrics to re-create original colours in tiles is part of the challenge and enjoyment of making floor-tile quilts. Sometimes, a particular design detail means that I will have to find a substitute and seeking a suitable alternative becomes a mission, if not an obsession. All Saints Church in Bristol has highly decorative tiles and a design that particularly appealed to me. I chose to substitute the ornate

**Below:** Bristol Cathedral tiles and (right) 'Autumnal Directions'

tile with a vibrant batik fabric that gives the quilt a special glow. (See page 46–53.)

I have written this book to share my fascination with floor-tile designs and I hope that the illustrations of floors and quilts will inspire you to make your own. Instructions follow for making several of the quilts shown but you can also use this book as a design resource and, who knows, perhaps it will inspire you to take your own journey along the patchwork pavement route, designing your own quilts inspired by tiled floors.

**Centre left**: 'Turning the Corner', inspired by the floor of the Ambleside chemist's shop. Detail top left
**Right**: 'Venetian Celebration' was based on the floor of St Mark's Venice (bottom left). Simpler alternatives are shown on page 99

# From Design to Reality

Decorative tiles and tile patterns can be found in many ecclesiastical buildings, but there are many other locations in which I have been pleasantly surprised to find them, including the porch or hall of friends' houses. Some older shops have them in the entranceway, as have banks, town halls and other municipal buildings built in the 19th century. Wherever you are travelling, whether in Europe, America or elsewhere in the world, take the opportunity to look at churches, abbeys and cathedrals, especially in Italy as here you will find many of the wonderful originals from which the Victorian industrialists took their inspiration.

## Making a Record

The most important piece of equipment you will need is a camera to record your special finds. It is important to ask permission, then photograph as much of the floor as you can, remembering to include any corners of the border designs – it can sometimes be rather difficult to work out how to get the border design of your quilt to turn the corner if you have no record (see 'Turning the Corner', page 80). In the past I have used print film but now I am turning to a digital camera to record my finds. Of course, that means that you have to have use of a computer and a good printer, and you will also need to know how to use them to good effect.

**Above:** Medallion floor at the altar of Bristol Cathedral

If it is not possible to photograph the tiles, keep a sketchbook with you so that you can sit down and draw the designs. Squared paper is ideal for this purpose and I have also found that because this process lasts longer than taking a photograph, I can get much more inspired as I think about how the pieces go together and how they relate to traditional patchwork designs.

## Choosing the Design

Once you have a record of the tile designs, you will need to study them carefully to decide which blocks will inspire you to make that special quilt. This will depend in part on how

complex or easy you want your design to be. You may decide to use just one block, or you could combine two or three. Perhaps a section of a pattern will appeal to you as the intricate Mariners Compass design on the altar floor of Bristol Cathedral did to Judy Mathieson. You will see that Judy used that design as the main inspiration for her wonderful award-winning quilt 'Bristol Stars' (above).

My own version of that central area was inspired by only one of the Mariner's Compasses, which I made in French Provençal fabrics as a medallion. I extended the borders and appliquéd on some teapots because I loved their clean designs. I called the quilt 'Tea Time 2' (overleaf).

You may be intrigued by border patterns – even an easy design adds more vitality to the edge of a quilt than a plain wide border. A common border design on both floor tiles and quilts is the 'Square on Point', which I have often used to good effect.

## Drafting the Design

Once you have chosen the blocks, you can use a computer software programme such as Electric Quilt or Quilt Pro to reproduce your quilt, but I prefer to sit with graph paper, pencil, pen and ruler to draft out the blocks to scale. In that way, I know precisely how the pieces will fit together. At that point I can also determine how large the blocks will be and can begin to envisage the eventual size of the quilt.

During this process you may decide to alter the design slightly, either because you feel that it will enhance the whole look or because the original tile pattern is too complicated for you. You also have the option of creating two quilts from the same design that will look completely different – one in the original tile colours and another in your favourite contemporary fabrics. Having chosen the basic block, you can draft several of them into a square of 3 x 3 blocks or 4 x 4 blocks. With tracing paper over the top and using a soft pencil to outline patterns, you can begin to see other secondary designs emerging that may determine your eventual use of different fabrics. I find

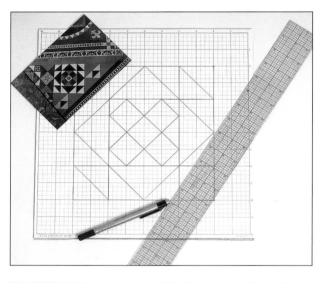

an additional benefit of using this technique is that you can begin to gauge the tonal values of light, medium and dark in your quilt.

## Choosing Fabrics

For me, the best part of the design process is choosing the fabrics. I have made a large collection of marbled fabrics in colours as close to the original tiles as possible. These include many batiks as they give the texture I am trying to re-create. I also use other cotton fabrics and sometimes I find that the exact colour I am looking for is on the back rather than the front – don't forget to turn the fabric over when you are looking for an exact match.

I find that stitching a quilt in colours as close to the floor design as possible makes me familiar with the blocks. While I am working on it, I can begin to envisage a tile-inspired quilt in contemporary colours. This is your springboard to changing the style and the setting of the blocks if you wish.

## Equipment

It is essential to work with good equipment that you are comfortable using. Most tile designs are made up of geometric shapes with points that need to match so you must be as accurate as possible in your cutting and piecing techniques.

# Sewing Basics

## Preparing Fabric

Making a collection of fabrics to create quilts inspired by floor tiles is a really enjoyable part of the process. It is essential to buy longer lengths than you might normally purchase and to buy when you see, otherwise you might not find the same fabric again. The colours used in floor-tile designs are usually terracotta, black, shades of brown, pink and cream with the addition of blue and green. I usually look out for fabrics giving the appearance of marble with a slight vein running randomly through them. Batiks are my fabrics of choice, together with marbled designs created by several other cotton fabric manufacturers.

The instructions for making the quilts in this book recommend cutting along the length of 44 inches, so it is preferable to buy long lengths rather than fat lengths. Some quilters wash their fabrics before sewing. I tend not to unless the quilt I am making is destined for a bed and the fabric will therefore have to be washed. If there is a particular fabric I think might run or shrink, I wash it gently with a special wool detergent, then

rinse several times. If it still continues to run, I will not use it. Generally, however, the way in which batik fabric is made involves washing and rinsing several times, and I have not experienced any problems with those fabrics.

## Rotary Cutting Equipment

For accurate cutting, good rotary cutting equipment is essential.

**Rulers**: It is easier and leads to fewer mistakes to cut with the correct width of ruler. I find the following sizes very useful: 2½in, 3½in, 4½in and 6½in. I also have a collection of squares in those sizes as well as much larger squares for squaring up the corners when the quilt is finished, prior to sewing on the binding. I use Creative Grids clear acrylic rulers (see photograph above) because I find the non-slip spots on the back help to make cutting accurate.

**Rotary Cutter**: Use one that is comfortable in your hand. Try out the various types at your local quilt shop or quilt show. A sharp blade brings greater accuracy to cutting.

**Cutting table**: Your cutting table should be at a comfortable height for you to use standing up so that you can exert gentle pressure on the board with the cutter and not get backache in the process. House bricks or blocks of wood can be used to raise your table to the correct height.

## Cutting Fabric

The instructions following are for right-handed quilters. Reverse the instructions if you are left-handed.

1. Press the fabric before cutting to eliminate any creases – these can severely alter the size of pieces.
2. Fold the fabric in half with the selvedge running top to bottom and place on the board, using a horizontal line as a straightedge guide.
3. When cutting strips, place the ruler of the correct width vertically on the board, to the right of the edge, and use the vertical lines on the board to match up top and bottom measurements. (Photo 1a) Always cut away from yourself and close the blade of the cutter as soon as you have cut the piece.
4. Holding the ruler down with your thumb and three fingers, place your little finger on the left edge of the ruler to stabilize it. Gently exert pressure on the cutter and cut away from yourself. (Photo 1b)
5. Turn the strip and repeat to cut the rough edge. (Photo 1c)
6. Turn the strip lengthways, horizontally across the board, using the line as a straightedge guide. Cut the pieces to the correct measurement. (Photo 1d)

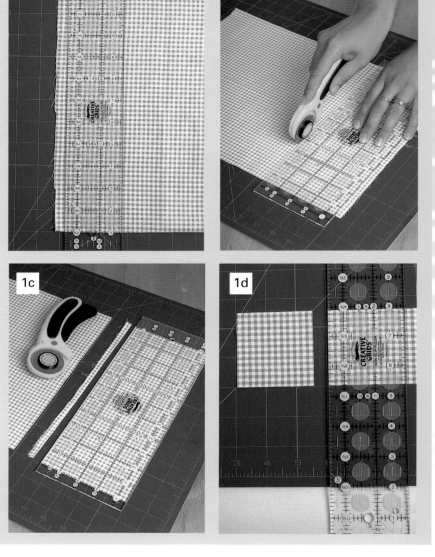

## Tip

You cannot make pieces wider if you cut them too small – always check your measurements before cutting.
Measure twice, cut once.

## Cutting Accurate Templates

Some of the designs in this book require you to cut plastic templates. Always use firm plastic and a permanent fine felt-tip pen for tracing and marking them.
1. Place the diagram to be traced on a flat surface and secure with masking tape.
2. Place your template plastic over the design and secure with masking tape.
3. Using a 1in wide ruler and the permanent pen, trace the design, making sure you are absolutely accurate. (Photo 2a)

4. Cut out the template with paper scissors or an old rotary cutting blade.
5. Mark the template with a coloured dot on the top to make sure you use the template the right way round. (Photo 2b) Add a name or letter to identify it.

## Sewing Machine

There are many makes of sewing machine from the simple to the elaborate electronic, computerised models. The main functions needed to make the quilts in this book are straight sewing, a good satin stitch with variable width and the ability to do free-motion quilting with the feed dogs down or covered. The Husqvarna Viking Designer 2 that I use also has a scissors function, a fix stitch for securing the stitching and a needle down function, all of which are extremely useful when piecing and quilting.

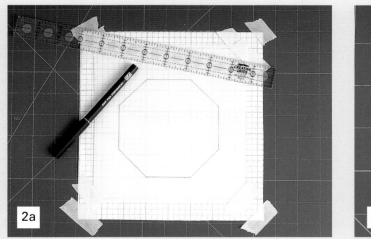

2a

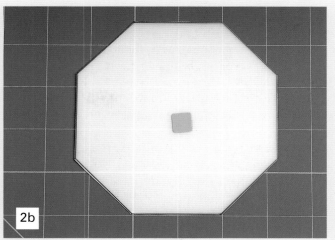

2b

## Feet Required

1. *¼in:* The ability to sew an accurate ¼in seam is essential for accuracy in piecing. Many machines now have their own-brand ¼in foot. For those that do not, there are now ¼in feet available to convert them. For details, ask your local dealer or a quilt shop which sells sewing machines.

2. *Open-toed foot*: It is easier and more accurate to sew a satin stitch if the foot used is open toed as this gives an instant view of the stitch.

3. *Darning foot*: When free-motion quilting, as when stippling, it is essential to use the correct foot for your machine. Some darning feet are open toed, others are made of a see-through plastic, but the most important feature is to be able to lower the feed dogs (or cover them up) so that you can manoeuvre the quilt sandwich freely as you quilt.

4. *Walking foot*: (Sometimes called the quilting foot.) On

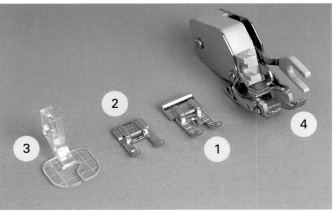

most machines this is a large foot with little feet beneath it that literally walk the quilt sandwich through the machine. This prevents puckers and tucks in the backing fabric. There are now open-toed walking feet available which give a better view as you stitch. Ask your dealer for details, giving the specifications of the make and model of your machine.

## Machine Needles

Change the needle frequently, particularly when sewing on batik and also when quilting. I recommend the following needle sizes:

*Size 70* for sewing on 100% cotton batik, which has a high weave count.

*Size 80* for sewing and piecing regular 100% cotton.

*Quilting sizes 75–90* for quilting.

*Embroidery sizes 75–90* for satin stitch work.

## Piecing

To join pieces accurately, pin them at both ends and in the centre so that any easing can take place in between. Always use a ¼in seam allowance. (Except when foundation piecing. See 'Venetian Celebration', page 96.)

Use matching thread where possible, otherwise a dark beige or mid-grey should work with most fabrics.

## Pressing

For accurate piecing it helps to press as you go. You are not ironing, but simply pressing. I use steam to get rid of creases and folds, otherwise a hot iron should be used to press seams to one side or open as you wish. A good iron and board at the right height, conveniently placed close to the sewing machine, helps enormously while piecing. I press my work as I go, to make sure that I have achieved perfect points and matching seams. It is far easier to rectify this at the piecing stage rather than later when the quilt top is completed.

## Fusing

Some chapters use fusing as a technique for adding fabric. Use a fusible web such as 'Bondaweb' or 'Steam a Seam', remembering that whichever side you trace on to, the image will turn out in reverse. Practice with one piece first to experiment. Use a warm to hot iron.

1. Trace the image on to fusible web and number it or give it a letter to avoid confusion later on.
2. Cut out the piece with a rough ¼in allowance all the way round. (Photo 3a)
3. Press the fusible web to the wrong side of the fabric, making sure that the edges do not go over the fabric and on to the ironing board. (Photo 3b).
4. Cut out the shape, peel off the backing paper and press with a warm to hot iron on to the fabric in the required position.
5. Secure the edges with a satin stitch.

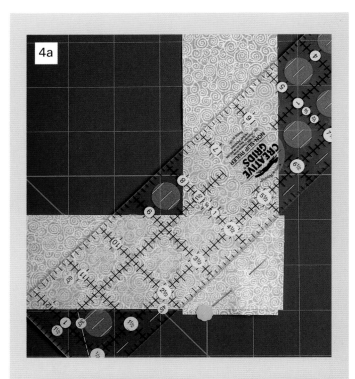

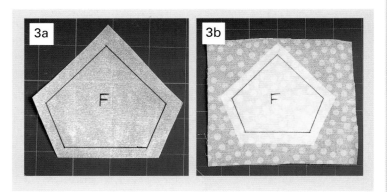

## Tip

There is a special fusible web pressing sheet that you can buy to prevent messing up your ironing board. Ask your local quilt shop for details.

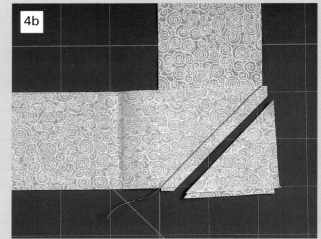

## Continuous Strips

Using this method for joining strips or to make a continuous strip for binding is very easy. It is less noticeable and also less bulky than sewing a straight seam.

1. Cut strips to the required width.
2. Place them right sides together, one horizontally and the other vertically.
3. Use a fabric marker to draw a line at 45°. (Photo 4a)
4. Sew along the line and cut away the waste. (Photo 4b)
5. Press the seam open. (Photo 4c)

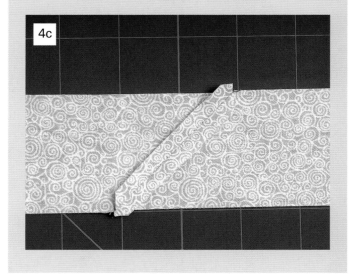

## Mitred Corners

When adding borders, a mitred corner gives a professional finish.

1. Measure the width of the quilt.
2. Cut border strips that measurement but add twice the width of the border plus 3in.
3. Fold the border strip in half and mark with a pin.
4. Divide your width measurement in half and measure that distance either side of the centre pin. Pin to the quilt.
5. Start and end the seam ¼in from both ends.
6. Add all the borders using this method.
7. Press the seam allowances towards the border strips.
8. Fold the quilt diagonally towards the corner so the border strips lie parallel and pin. Draw a line at 45° from the end of the border seam. (Fig 5a)
9. Sew along that line from the corner to the edge and trim away the waste. (Fig 5b)
10. Press the seam open. (Fig 5c)

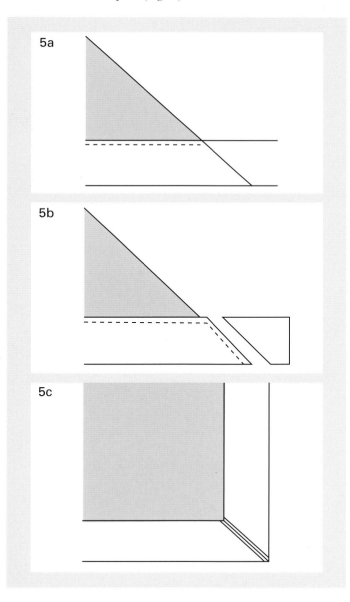

## Marking the Quilt Design

You may wish to mark the quilt before assembling the quilt sandwich. If you are free-motion machining, you have no need to do this. If you have decided to use a simple grid design – and some of the tile quilts lend themselves to this – you can mark the lines when the quilt sandwich is made. If machine quilting, try to use continuous designs to prevent too many stops and starts.

There are many different quilting design sources available, from stencils to books of continuous patterns. You may have to enlarge or reduce them and make your own stencils by tracing through template plastic. You may even wish to incorporate a design you have seen in the building from which the original tiles came.

Choose the marker carefully, making sure on spare pieces of the fabric you have used in the quilt that you can remove the marks. There are many different types of quilt-marking pen and pencil available. I prefer to use chalk pencils because I know I can remove the marks with an old toothbrush without wetting the quilt.

Another method of applying the quilting design is to trace it on to paper to make sure you have the exact size, then, using greaseproof paper, cut it the length of the stencil and fold it into as many folds as it will take. Press firmly. Using an old machine needle and a high number of stitches per inch, pin the stencil on to the greaseproof paper and machine around the design. You can then cut the folds in the paper and pin the designs to your quilt top. Then just machine along the lines. It will be easy to remove the greaseproof paper as you have already machined along the lines.

## Making the Quilt Sandwich

This stage is crucial to the finished look of your quilt. Care taken now will give you a quilt to be proud of.

1. Press the quilt top and measure the width and the length.
2. Add 4–6in to this measurement and cut the backing and batting to that size. You may have to piece the backing. If so, take care to avoid a centre seam.
3. Fold the backing in half and place a pin to mark the halfway point on each side. Lay out the backing with the wrong side facing uppermost and with the pins at the halfway points showing. If using a table, secure the backing to it with masking tape at several points along the edges, smoothing it out until it is flat. If using the floor, pin along the edges, making sure it is flat.
4. In the same way fold the batting in half and place a pin to mark the halfway point on each side. Lay the batting on top of the backing, matching the halfway pins. Gently smooth out the batting.
5. Fold the quilt top in half and place pins to mark the halfway point on each side. Lay it over the batting, matching the halfway pins. Smooth it out to get rid of any creases.
6. You are now ready to use your preferred method of

keeping the quilt sandwich together. If you are hand quilting, tack (baste) the layers together in a grid about 4in apart, using a contrasting thread. If machine quilting you can place 1in safety pins at frequent intervals across the quilt. (No larger, or you risk putting holes in the quilt.) If you are using a quilt tack gun, place a grid underneath and fire the tacks at frequent intervals. There are also quilt-basting sprays available, and you will have to apply the spray to each layer as you assemble the quilt sandwich.

## Attaching Binding

All the quilts in this book are finished with binding. It frames the quilt and gives a neat finish.

1. Cut strips 2½in wide and join in a continuous strip as explained on page 16. (The number of strips required is listed in the Cutting section for each quilt.)

2. Press in half lengthways.

3. Press one end of the binding diagonally and trim away, leaving a generous ¼in.

4. Place the raw edge of the binding a scant ¼in in from the raw edge of the quilt, starting about halfway along one side. Check that there isn't a seam in the continuous strip at the corner, then pin the binding in place. (Fig 6a)

5. Using a ¼in seam allowance, start sewing about 3in further from the diagonal fold on the binding and stop a ¼in from the corner. Sew diagonally into the corner. (This is a useful tip I picked up from Libby Lehmann.) (Fig 6b)

6. Fold the binding up. (Fig 6c)

7. Fold down the binding parallel with the edge and sew the next side, starting from the top of the quilt and maintaining the ¼in seam allowance. (Fig 6d)

8. Continue until all the corners have been sewn.

9. When you come towards your start point, cut the binding to just more than the diagonal fold at the starting point and tuck the rest of the binding into the fold. Pin it firmly into place and sew down.

10. From the front of the quilt, press the binding away from the edge, using a medium-hot iron. Take care if you have used a polyester thread as this will melt.

11. Cut ¼in wide strips of Bondaweb or Steam a Seam and press them on to the seam allowance from the back of the quilt. (Fig 6e)

12. Peel off the paper and press the binding down to the back of the quilt, taking care to mitre the corners.

13. Sew the two binding ends firmly into the diagonal seam.

14. Hem the binding in place. (Fig 6f)

## Stitching in the Ditch

I find it helps to stabilize the quilt sandwich if I stitch along all the seams before stitching my chosen quilting design. This is known as stitching in the ditch.

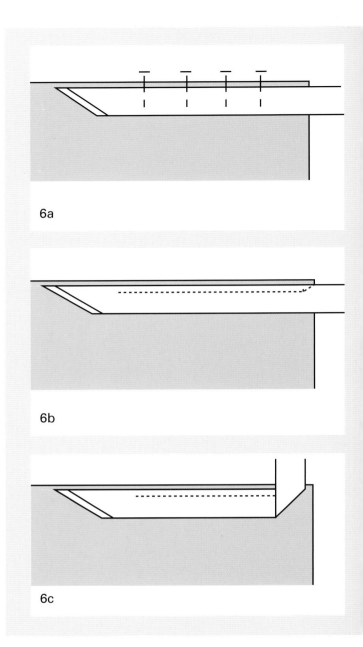

6a

6b

6c

## Attaching a Hanging Sleeve

Many of the quilts in this book are wall hangings rather than bed quilts. This method of attaching a hanging sleeve will ensure that the quilt will hang well.

1. Measure the width of the quilt.

2. Cut a 9½in wide strip of your sleeve fabric the width of the quilt. (Fig 7a)

3. Turn in ½in on the short edges, fold over again and machine down. (Fig 7b)

4. Fold wrong sides together, pin the ends together and then centre and sew ½in from the edge. (Fig 7c)

5. Fold the tube in half lengthways and press the seam in the middle of the back. (Fig 7d)

6. Pin the hanging sleeve with the seam at the back, to the top of the quilt, just below the binding. Attach the top edge

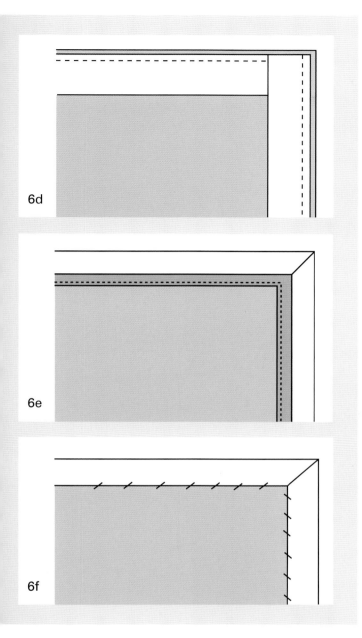

6d

6e

6f

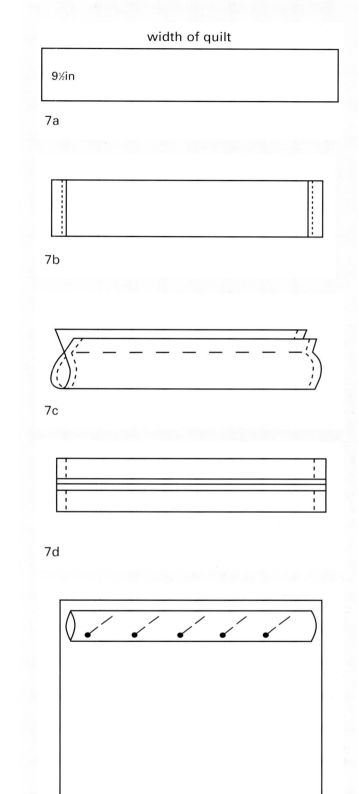

width of quilt

9½in

7a

7b

7c

7d

7e

of the sleeve to the quilt with small stitches that do not show on the front. Remove the pins. (Fig 7e)

**7.** Push the top of the sleeve up about ½in to just below the top of the quilt and pin to the quilt again. Hem the bottom edge of the sleeve to the quilt with small stitches that do not show on the front. Remove the pins.

**8.** Sew a label to the bottom-left corner of the back of the quilt, recording your name, the title of the quilt and the date you made it.

## Note

For clarity, no seam allowances are included in any of the diagrams in this book.

# Quilt Projects

My fascination with floor-tile
designs has inspired me to create many quilts.
Here are some projects for you to make, from the
simple progressing to the more complex, from
small wall hangings to large quilts.
Enjoy making your own quilts
inspired by the floors beneath
your feet.

# Johnsons' Floor

**Above:** 'Johnsons' Floor'
66in x 66in

A recent visit to friends held a delightful surprise, for in the porch of their Victorian villa was a perfect set of floor tiles. The 'Variable Star' block was a popular choice for tiled Victorian floors and here, with its variation of inverted 'Flying Geese' in the outer centres, it produces a secondary design of a 'Square Within a Square'. This fine example shows a peach centre square on point, surrounded by black triangles, which in turn are surrounded by dark beige and white 'Flying Geese' with chocolate brown corner squares. But what set this design apart from others are the sashing strips that bisect the main blocks. Brick red strips either side of the central peach strip frame the blocks and at the point where they meet is a small white-and-black nine-patch block. This provides a foil for the other colours and brings symmetry to the whole design.

**Top left**: A block of the porch floor
**Top right**: Detail of the finished quilt
**Bottom**: The Johnsons' porch floor

When I set out to make this quilt I decided to set the whole design on point to see whether I could make the quilt more interesting while at the same time retaining the feeling of the floor. By adding side setting triangles in peach to create a square, I was able to add the inner border and echo the black-and-white nine-patch block in the corners. In this way I could show all the elements of the floor together. The outer border sets off the whole thing. It combines a dark chocolate frame with cream squares on point flanked by beige triangles.

The configuration of this quilt is very popular for the border treatment of decorative floors, as it is indeed for borders of quilts. On this particular floor there is a further border that I chose to alter slightly and make with brick red and peach strip sets to echo the frame surrounding the central blocks. I wanted to give this quilt a textural quality and decided to use the trapunto method described by Harri Walner in her book, *Trapunto by Machine*. Sandie Lush created the feather design for me, highlighting the larger peach setting triangles.

**Above**: The Johnsons' house
**Below left and right**: Details of the quilt, showing the trapunto feather quilting design

**Above:** 'Summer Garden' 28in x 28in quilted by Beryl Cadman

## 'Summer Garden' Quilt

For the contemporary version of this quilt there were several elements I could have chosen to repeat from the original design – the nine-patch, the 'Variable Star' block or the diamond border. Inspired by the five 'Variable Star' blocks that make up the centre of the main quilt and some flowers in our garden, I added some extra elements and created a small wall hanging. This quilt includes four-patch units in the centres of the outer blocks and half-square triangles in the corners of these same blocks. Inspired by the bright fabrics, I 'fussy cut' the inner squares from a border print to give a more symmetrical look. The placement of light, medium and dark values emphasizes different elements in this pretty quilt.

# Johnsons' Floor

## MATERIALS

### Fabric

A variety of 100% cotton fabrics
44in wide in colours to represent
the tiles:
2 yards peach
1 yard chocolate brown
½ yard light brown
1 yard cream
½ yard mid-brown
2 yards brick red
1¼ yards black
¼ yard white
1 yard beige

### Batting

72in x 72in of your choice

### Backing

4 yards of your choice

**Fabric marking pens or pencils,
light and dark**

**¼ yard freezer paper**

**Large square ruler**

## CUTTING *Measurements include ¼in seam allowances*

### Peach

2 squares (16in). Cut in half
  diagonally
2 squares (14in). Cut in half
  diagonally
5 squares (6½in)
15 strips (1½in wide)

### Chocolate brown

2 strips (3½in wide). Cut into
  20 squares (3½in)
11 strips (1¾in wide)

### Light brown

3 strips (3½in wide). Cut into
  20 rectangles (3½in x 6½in)

### Cream

4 strips (3½in wide). Cut into
  40 squares (3½in)
5 strips (2½in wide). Cut into
  80 squares (2½in)

1 strip (1¾in wide). Cut into
  16 squares (1¾in)

### Mid brown

3 strips (3½in wide). Cut into
  24 squares (3½in)

### Brick red

30 strips (1½in wide)

### Black

3 strips (1½in wide)
6 strips (2½in wide) for binding

### White

3 strips (1½in wide)

### Beige

11 strips (2½in wide). Cut into
  172 squares (2½in)

## BLOCK ASSEMBLY

### Block 1: 12in square

**1.** Use a fabric marker pen to draw a diagonal line across the wrong side of all the 3½in cream squares.

**2.** Place a cream square on the left corner of a 6½in x 3½in light brown rectangle and stitch on the marked line. (Fig 1a)

**3.** Cut the surplus ¼in from the stitch line. (Fig 1b)

**4.** Fold back the cream fabric and press. (Fig 1c)

**5.** Repeat on the opposite corner. (Fig 1d)

**6.** Make four identical units.

**7.** Use a light fabric marker pen to draw a diagonal line across the wrong side of all the 3½in chocolate brown squares.

**8.** Place a chocolate brown square on the left-hand corner of each 6½in peach square and machine along the marked line. Cut the surplus ¼in from the stitch line.

**9.** Fold back the chocolate brown fabric and press.

**10.** Repeat on the opposite corner and then the remaining two corners.

**11.** Lay out one peach-and-brown unit, four brown-and-cream units and four 3½in mid brown squares as shown in the diagram and sew together in rows. (Fig 1e)

**12.** Stitch the rows together to make the block.

**13.** Make five blocks.

Fig 1e

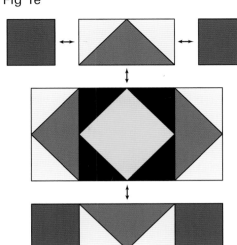

### Block 2: 3in square

**1.** Join one 1½in black strip to each long edge of one 1½in white strip. Cut across the width into strips 1½in wide. (Fig.2a)

**2.** Sew one 1½in white strip to each long edge of one 1½in black strip. Cut across the width of the joined fabric into strips 1½in wide as before. (Fig 2b)

**3.** Sew the nine-patch units together as shown. (Fig 2c)

**4.** Make 16 nine-patch blocks.

### Strip Sets

**1.** Stitch a 1½in brick red strip to each long edge of each 1½in peach strip.

**2.** Cut 16 pieces 12½in long across the width (the remaining strips will be used for the borders). (Fig 3)

### Inner Quilt Assembly

**1.** Lay out the blocks, strip sets and large peach triangles as shown overleaf. Place 16in peach triangles at the sides and 14in peach triangles at the corners. (Fig 4)

**2.** Sew together in rows.

**3.** Draw four 3in squares on the freezer paper and cut out.

**4.** Centre a freezer-paper square on a 3½in mid brown square, shiny side up. There will be a ¼in seam allowance all the way round. Repeat with the remaining three paper squares.

**5.** With a very warm iron, turn the seam allowance to the back and press it gently along the edge of the paper.

**6.** Place the four fabric squares on the four side setting triangles as

Fig 1a

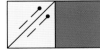

Fig 1b

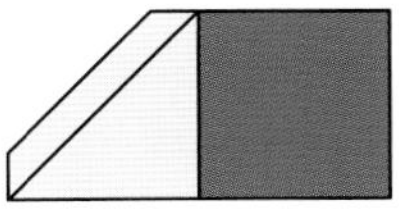

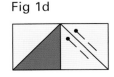

Fig 1c

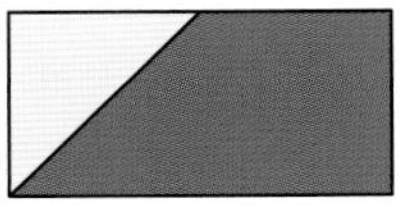

Fig 1d

Fig 2a

Fig 2b

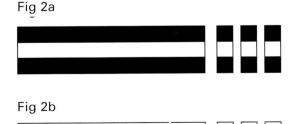

Fig 2c

Fig 3

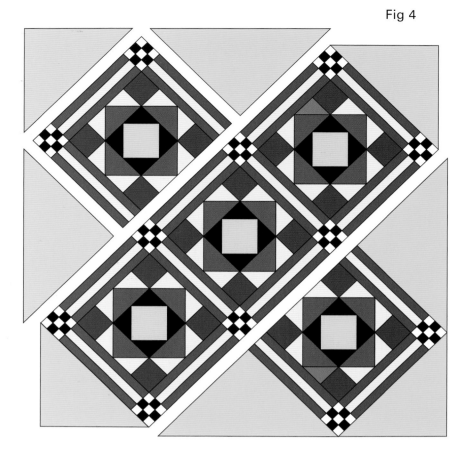
Fig 4

8. Trim the edges carefully, leaving a seam allowance of just over ¼in. (Fig 5c)
9. Sew a strip to the top and bottom edges of the quilt.
10. To make the four corner squares, draw a diagonal line across the wrong side of the 1¾in cream squares.
11. Attach one 1¾in cream square to each corner of the four remaining 2½in beige square following steps 1–4 for Block 1.
12. Sew a corner square to each end of the two remaining Seminole strip sets.
13. Sew these strips to the two opposite sides of the quilt.
14. Measure across the centre of the quilt and make up two chocolate brown strips the same measurement.
15. Sew a strip to the bottom and top of the quilt and press outwards.
16. Measure down the centre of the quilt, including the chocolate brown strips, and cut two more strips the same measurement.
17. Sew the strips to the sides of the quilt and press outwards.

### Border 3

1. Measure across the centre of the quilt top. Cut four units the same measurement plus 8in of the red-peach-red strip sets. (The extra is for mitring the corners.)
2. Place a pin in the centre and measure half the width measurement either side. Place pins as markers and then pin along the length of the quilt to ¼in from the ends.
3. Sew a strip set to the bottom and top of the quilt and press outwards.
4. Repeat steps 1–2 above for the two remaining sides and sew these two strips to the sides of the quilt top. (Fig 6)
5. Mitre the corners of the border strips. (See Sewing Basics, page 17, for details.)

shown in the finished quilt and press them in place.
7. Neatly hand appliqué the squares in place.
8. From the back of the quilt, carefully cut away the peach fabric from behind the appliquéd mid brown squares and remove the freezer paper.
9. With a large square ruler, (I use a 20½in square) square up the corners of the quilt and then the edges, leaving a ¼in seam allowance all the way round.

### Border 1

1. Measure across the centre of the quilt top. Cut four lengths of the peach-and-red strip sets to the same measurement.
2. Sew a strip set to the bottom and top of the quilt and press outwards.
3. Sew a nine-patch black-and-white block to each end of the remaining two strips.

4. Sew these two strips to the sides of the quilt top.

### Border 2

1. Measure down the centre of the quilt. Make up two 1¾in chocolate brown strips to the same measurement.
2. Sew a strip to the two sides of the quilt and press outwards.
3. Measure across the centre of the quilt, including the chocolate brown strips. Cut two more strips the same measurement.
4. Sew the strips to the top and bottom of the quilt and press outwards.
5. Join the 2½in beige squares and the 2½in cream squares into 80 strip sets. (Fig 5a)
6. Join these sets into four units of twenty strips, Seminole style. (Fig 5b)
7. Stitch a beige square to the free edge of each cream end square.

Fig 5a

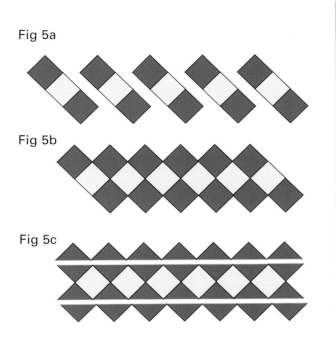

Fig 5b

Fig 5c

Fig 6

## QUILTING AND FINISHING

### Backing

**1.** Cut and join the backing fabric to fit the quilt, overlapping by 2in all the way round. Press any seams open.
**2.** Cut the batting to exactly the same size.

### Quilting

**1.** Make the quilt sandwich of top, batting and backing and secure with safety pins, quilt tacks or basting spray if machine quilting, or by tacking if hand sewing. (See Sewing Basics, page 17.)
**2.** Quilt as desired. I quilted in the ditch along most of the seams to stabilize the blocks and worked minimal decorative quilting because I felt the design spoke for itself.

### Binding

**1.** Measure the perimeter of the quilt. Join 2½in wide strips of black fabric in a continuous strip to fit.
**2.** Fold in half along the length and iron flat.
**3.** Refer to Sewing Basics, page 18, for details of attaching the binding.

### Label

Make a label for the back, giving details of the name of your quilt, the date you finished it, your name and the town you live in.

### Hanging Sleeve

Refer to Sewing Basics, page 18, for details of attaching the hanging sleeve.

# *Chocolate Symphony*

The centre of the city of
Bristol still contains 14
churches within a quarter
square mile. Most date back to the
14th century and over the years
they have been subject to
renovation and change to match
passing fads and fancies and the
tastes of the incumbent clerics. St
Stephen's Church had its floor tiles
laid in the 19th century. The
flagstones that formed the original
floor also acted as covers for burial
sites. When the Victorians laid the
tiles on top of the flags, they
marked the sites of the tombs with
numbers that can be clearly seen
within the terracotta patterns.

**Left**: 'Chocolate Symphony'
44in x 77½in

The pattern of the tiles in the main aisle is a dark brown and cream 'Square Within a Square' surrounded, 'Log Cabin' style, by brick red. Set on point, these blocks have a band of narrow black sashing between them with cream corner squares. A wider border frames the main body of the floor pattern with cream and brick red 'Flying Geese' that provide an attractive feature in their own right and help to set off the centre design.

I felt that the whole design was strong and forceful, and required some equally distinctive fabrics so I followed the design and colour scheme as closely as possible. Once completed, the chocolate tones of the main fabric stood out, inspiring the name of the quilt, 'Chocolate Symphony'.

**Left**: 'Flying Geese' tile border
**Below**: Quilted 'Flying Geese'
**Bottom**: 'Chocolate Symphony' beside the tiles that inspired it

**Left**: St Stephen's Church
**Below**: Detail of the tiles beside the font
**Below left**: Arthur Maw's archive catalogue
tile design

The floor around the font in the Baptistery at the west end of the church has a completely different design that bears no relation to the aisle patterns. The font covers the central area, but the rest of the design is identical to a pattern featured in the Arthur Maw catalogue that I saw in the Jackfield Tile Museum. The popular 'Square Within a Square' is used in two different colourways, red, white and black making up an attractive maze-like symmetrical pattern with green and black as a centre border motif. 'Variable Stars' in green, cream and red, placed on point and joined in a row, make an unusual inner border. An extra outer border of green and black triangles completes this attractive design.

**Above:** 'Cat on a Hot Tiled Roof'
57in x 57in

## A Feast for the Eye

With the advent of grandchildren in our family, some character fabrics were called for and I decided to make a vibrant and stimulating quilt from my collection of cat fabrics for little eyes to feast upon. By making the quilt square rather than rectangular, as in the original design, I was able to have more blocks in which to feature the different cats. The sashing needed to be outstanding to compete with the rich primary colours of the main blocks, and I found that a selection of spotty fabrics brought additional vitality and colour to this quilt. The 'Flying Geese' border was turned to go along the quilt edge rather than running perpendicular to it and is made up of half-square triangles. Brightly coloured striped fabric cut on the bias made the ideal binding to complete the look.

# Chocolate Symphony

## MATERIALS

### Fabric
A variety of 100% cotton fabrics
44in wide in colours to represent
the tiles:
½ yard dark brown
3 yards brick red
2 yards cream
1¼ yards black

### Binding
1 yard mid brown

### Batting
50in x 84in 100% cotton

### Backing
2½ yards of your choice

### Fabric marker pen

### Extra rulers
Square: 5½in, 15½in (optional)

## CUTTING *Measurements include ¼in seam allowances*

### Dark brown
3 strips (4in wide). Cut into
  22 squares (4in)

### Brick red
16 strips (3in wide). Cut into
  32 rectangles (3in x 10½in);
  20 rectangles (3in x 5½in);
  12 rectangles (3in x 8in)
8 strips (4½in wide). Cut into
  98 rectangles (4½in x 2½in);
  4 squares (4½in)
2 strips (3in wide). Cut into
  28 squares (3in)

### Cream
4 strips (3½in wide). Cut into
  38 squares (3½in)
14 strips (2½in wide). Cut into
  212 squares (2½in)
1 strip (1¾in wide). Cut into
  23 squares (1¾in)
6 strips (2½in wide) for binding

### Black
21 strips (1¾in wide). Cut into
  32 rectangles (1¾in x 10½in);
  8 rectangles (1¾in x 4½in). The
  remainder is for the sashing

## BLOCK ASSEMBLY

### Block 1: 10in

**1.** Cut the 3½in cream squares in half diagonally to make 76 triangles.

**2.** Sew a cream triangle to one side of a 4in dark brown square and press outwards. (Fig 1a)

**3.** Repeat on the opposite edge and then on the remaining two sides. (Fig 1b)

**4.** Make ten of these 'Square Within a Square' blocks.

**5.** Use a 5½in square ruler to square up the blocks to 5½in square, including a ¼in seam allowance all the way round.

**6.** Sew a 3in x 5½in brick red rectangle to opposite sides of a 'Square Within a Square' block and press outwards. (Fig 1c)

**7.** Sew a 3in x 10½in brick red rectangle to the two remaining sides. (Fig 1d)

**8.** Make ten blocks.

### Block 2

**1.** Sew a cream triangle on to one side of a dark brown square as in step 1 above.

**2.** Now add a cream triangle to the two adjacent sides. (Fig 2a)

**3.** Make 12 blocks.

**4.** Square up the two outer sides as in step 5 above.

**5.** Sew a 3in brick red square to each cream side triangle. (Fig 2b)

**6.** Sew a 3in x 8in brick red rectangle to one side of the block. (Fig 2c)

**7.** Sew a 3in x 10½in brick red rectangle to the remaining side. (Fig 2d)

**8.** Make 12 blocks.

### Quilt Assembly

**1.** Lay out the blocks, 1¾in cream squares and 1¾in x 10½in black rectangles as in the finished quilt (see left).

**2.** Join the blocks and strips in diagonal rows. (Fig 3 overleaf)

**3.** Join the rows together.

**4.** Use a large square ruler to square up the corners and a long ruler to trim the edges neatly, leaving a ¼in seam allowance all the way round.

### Border

**1.** Use a fabric marker pen to draw a diagonal line across the wrong side of all the 2½in cream squares.

**2.** Place a cream square on the left corner of a 4½in x 2½in red brick rectangle and machine stitch from corner to corner along the marked line. (Fig 4a overleaf)

**3.** Cut the surplus ¼in from the stitch line. (Fig 4b)

**4.** Fold back the cream fabric and press. (Fig 4c)

**5.** Repeat on the opposite corner. (Fig 4d)

**6.** Make 96 'Flying Geese' blocks.

**7.** Sew them into two strips of 16 and two strips of 33. (Note: you may need to add an extra 'Flying Geese' unit, depending on the length of your quilt.

Fig 1a

Fig 1b

Fig 1c

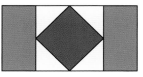

Fig 1d

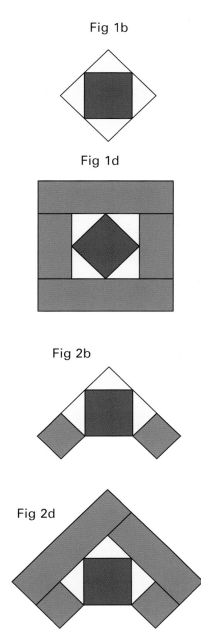

Fig 2a

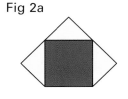

Fig 2b

Fig 2c

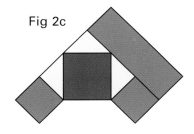

Fig 2d

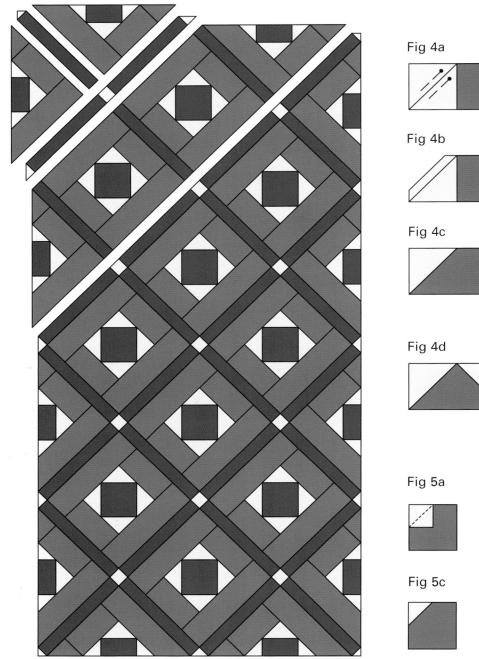

Fig 3

Fig 4a

Fig 4b

Fig 4c

Fig 4d

Fig 5a

Fig 5b

Fig 5c

Fig 5d

### Border Corners

**1**. Place a 2½in cream square on the left-hand corner of a 4½in red brick square and machine stitch along the marked line. (Fig 5a)
**2**. Cut the surplus ¼in from the stitch line. (Fig 5b)
**3**. Fold back the cream fabric and press. (Fig 5c)
**4**. Repeat on the opposite corner and then the remaining two corners. (Fig 5d)
**5**. Make four 'Square Within a Square' blocks.

### Sashing

**1**. Join the 1¾in black strips in a continuous piece. (See Sewing Basics, page 16.)
**2**. Measure the length of the quilt from top to bottom through the centre and cut four black strips to that length. This should be the same measurement as the length of the 33-strip 'Flying Geese' borders.
**3**. Sew a black strip to each long edge of each of the 33-strip 'Flying Geese' borders. Press outwards. Attach to the quilt.

**4.** Sew a 1¾in x 4½in black rectangle to opposite sides of the four 'Square Within a Square' blocks.

**5.** Sew a 'Square Within a Square' block to both ends of the two 16-strip 'Flying Geese' borders. (Fig 6)

**6.** Measure the width across the centre of the quilt and cut four 1¾in black strips that length. Stitch one to each long edge of each 16-strip 'Flying Geese' border. Press outwards.

**7.** Sew the border strips to the quilt and press outwards.

## QUILTING AND FINISHING

### Backing

**1.** Cut and join the backing fabric to fit the quilt, overlapping by 2in all the way round. Press any seams open.

**2.** Cut the batting to exactly the same size.

### Quilting

**1.** Make the quilt sandwich of top, batting and backing, and secure with safety pins, quilt tacks or basting spray if machine quilting, or by tacking if hand sewing. (See Sewing Basics, page 17.)

**2.** Quilt as desired. I stitched in the ditch along most of the seams to stabilize the blocks and created a chequerboard grid in the blocks. I stipple quilted around the cream centres of the blocks and the cream 'Flying Geese' triangles.

### Binding

**1.** Measure the perimeter of the quilt and join 2½in wide strips of cream fabric in a continuous strip to fit. (See page 16.)

**2.** Fold in half along the length and iron flat.

**3.** Refer to Sewing Basics, page 18, for details of attaching the binding.

### Label

Make a label for the back, giving details of the name of your quilt, the date you finished it, your name and the town you live in.

### Hanging Sleeve

Refer to Sewing Basics, page 18, for details of attaching the hanging sleeve.

Fig 6

# *Clifton Stars*

**Above:** 'Clifton Stars' 33in x 33in

In the elegant suburb of Clifton, close to the centre of Bristol, there are some stunning examples of Georgian and Victorian architecture. One of these fine buildings is home to a gentlemen's club called the Clifton Club. In the entrance hall corner is a perfect '54.40 or Fight' block in a bold configuration of terracotta, cream and black tiles, and this was my inspiration for the first quilt in a series of three. (If you are wondering about the name of the block, it comes from the middle of the 19th century when the United States and Canada were in dispute over the western, and final, stretch of the border between the two countries.)

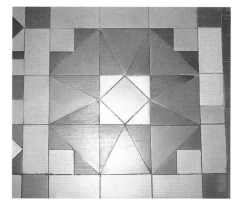

**Left:** Borders defining the thresholds to other rooms at the Clifton Club
**Centre left:** '54:40 or Fight' tile block
**Below:** First-floor hall of the Clifton Club, Bristol

The first-floor reception hall of the Clifton Club is covered almost entirely with triangles and squares in cream, terracotta and black. There are also other designs forming an elaborate series of borders across the thresholds to other rooms. These include the popular 'Square on Point' border.

The 'Ohio Star' block stands out with four cream corner squares and a central black square, with the nine-patch completed with alternate quarter-square triangles of terracotta and cream. On close examination, I saw that the floor had been laid with 'Square Within a Square' patterns, alternating cream and black with terracotta and black (see below). I certainly wanted to incorporate that in my final quilt design.

I first made the '54:40 or Fight' block in the original colours (near right) and decided to see whether combining that block with another would give me a secondary design. I chose a version of the 'Treasure Chest' block that I found in the hall of John and Sheila Waterfield's home, which would divide into a nine-patch block (below right). In order to make the star block stand out, I designed it to go in the centre and at the four corners of the quilt with the second block filling in the gaps in between.

By careful placement of dark, medium and light values of marbled fabrics a secondary design appeared that still retains the look of a tiled floor, and by extending triangles into the border becomes a design in its own right. By placing a 'Square Within a Square' in the corners of the quilt I was able to echo the centre of all nine blocks and the pattern on the first floor of the Clifton Club.

**Top**: The Clifton Club
**Centre left**: '54:40 or Fight' sample block; the block in the finished quilt is shown centre right
**Bottom left**: The 'Treasure Chest' quilt block with the tile block shown bottom right

## Developing New Ideas

Once I had my basic design I started playing with moving around all the dark, medium and light values until I came up with a completely different look. By placement of the dark colours I gave the illusion of curved piecing although all the pieces have straight lines. My second quilt, which I named 'Arrandarra', was made in the monochrome tones of turquoise (bottom right) while the third in the series, 'Purple Prose', combined purples with turquoise (top right). This time I emphasized the design from corner to corner across the quilt by using the pink/lavender/purple range. Once again, by extending the dark central triangles into the centre of the borders, I created a frame and focus for the whole design.

**Above right**: 'Purple Prose' 44in x 44in quilted by Beryl Cadman
**Above, centre**: Detail of 'Purple Prose'
**Right**: 'Arrandarra' 44in x 44in

# Clifton Stars

## MATERIALS

### Fabric
A variety of 100% cotton fabrics 44in wide in colours to represent the tiles:
1 yard pale peach
½ yard dark grey
½ yard black
½ yard white
½ yard yellow
¼ yard pale green
⅛ yard pale grey
⅛ yard brick red

### Fabric marker pen or chalk

### 'Tall Triangles Ruler Set'
Creative Grids (UK) Ltd or Tri-Recs Tools (EZ Wrights) Alternatively use a sheet of template plastic and a black permanent felt-tip pen

### Batting
38in square 100% cotton

### Backing
38in square of your choice

### 3½in square ruler

## CUTTING *Measurements include ¼in seam allowances*

**Pale peach**
20 squares (2in)
4 squares (3⅞in). Cut in half diagonally
8 strips (3½in x 15in)

**Dark grey**
5 squares (3½in)
8 strips (4¾in x 2⅝in)
1 strip (3½in x 18in). Cut 4 of template A (page 44)

**Black**
2 strips (3½in x 36in). Cut 20 of template B and 20 in reverse (fold the fabric to cut these simultaneously)
4 strips (2½in x 38in)

**White**
1 strip (3½in x 36in). Cut 20 of template A
8 strips (4¾in x 2⅝in)
16 squares (2in)

**Yellow**
10 squares (3⅞in). Cut in half diagonally
8 squares (2in). Cut in half diagonally
4 squares (3½in)

**Pale green**
14 squares (3⅞in). Cut in half diagonally

**Pale grey**
4 squares (4¾in)

**Brick red**
16 squares (2⅝in)

## BLOCK ASSEMBLY

I used an acrylic set of triangles for accuracy in cutting and piecing the black star points. Templates are given here for you to make your own.

### Block 1: 9in square

**1.** Use a fabric marker pen to draw a diagonal line across the wrong side of all the 2in pale peach squares.

**2.** Place a 2in pale peach square exactly across the corner of a 3½in dark grey square, right sides together.

**3.** Sew along the marked line and then trim off the corner, leaving an approximate ¼in seam allowance. Repeat on the opposite corner. (Fig 1a)

**4.** Press the corner triangles back. (Fig 1b)

**5.** Repeat on the remaining two opposite corners. Press the corner triangles back. (Fig 1c)

**6.** Use a 3½in acrylic square to make sure that the block is 3½in square and that there is a ¼in seam allowance all the way round the centre square.

**7.** Join one black triangle (B) to a white triangle (A). Join the reverse black triangle to the opposite side of A and trim off the bottom points. Press towards the outside of A. (Fig 1d)

**8.** Make three more of these units for this block.

**9.** With right sides together, join a 3⅞in pale green triangle to a 3⅞in yellow triangle. (Fig 1e)

**10.** Press the triangle open. Repeat to make three more of these small blocks. (Fig 1f)

**11.** Join your pieces together as shown to make your first block. Now make four more identical blocks. (Fig 1g)

### Block 2: 9in square

**1.** Using the pale grey and brick red squares, make the centre units following steps 1–5 for Block 1.

**2.** Square up the block to 4¾in square, making sure you have a ¼in seam allowance all the way round the centre square.

**3.** Sew a white and dark grey 4¾in x 2⅝in strip to opposite sides of the square unit and press outwards.

**4.** Sew a pale peach triangle to the white edge and a pale green triangle to the dark grey edge. (Fig 2a)

**5.** Sew a small yellow triangle to each end of the remaining white and dark grey 4¾in x 2⅝in strips.

**6.** Sew a pale peach triangle to one long edge of each of these white strips. Sew a pale green triangle to one long edge of each of these dark grey strips, as shown. (Fig 2b)

**7.** Sew these triangular units to opposite sides of the centre strip. Make three more identical blocks. (Fig 2c)

Fig 2a

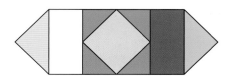

Fig 1a

Fig 1b

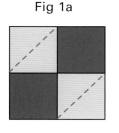

Fig 1c

Fig 1d

Fig 1e

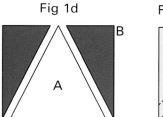

Fig 1f

Fig 1g

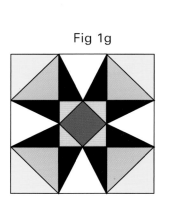

Fig 2b

Fig 2c

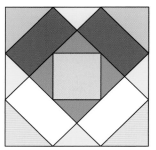

43

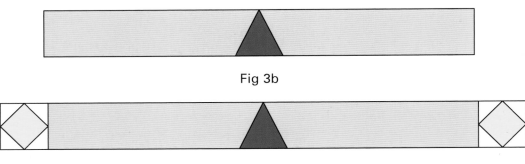

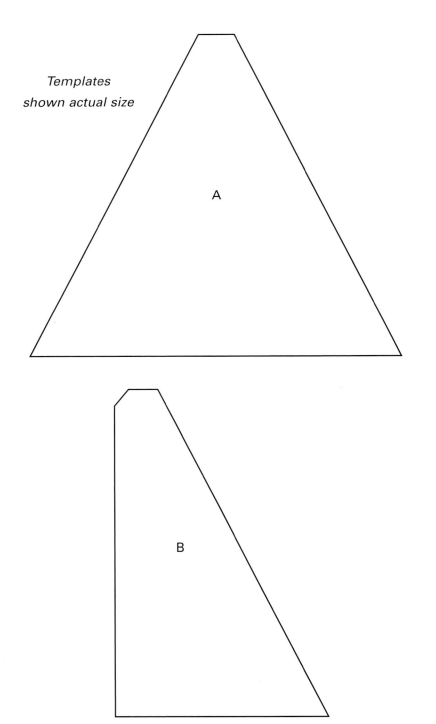

*Templates
shown actual size*

A

B

## Borders

**1**. Place template B on the right-hand end of a 3½in x 15in pale peach strip and cut the angle along the edge. Make three more.
**2**. Repeat on four more strips at the left-hand end so you have four sets, as shown. The dark grey triangles (A) should fit between the strip pairs. (Fig 3a)
**3**. Sew a dark grey triangle (A) to the centre of each set of strips.
**4**. Make four 'Square Within a Square' units following steps 1–5 for Block 1 using the 3½in yellow squares and 2in white squares.
**5**. Sew a 'Square Within a Square' unit to each end of two border strips. (Fig 3b)

## Quilt Assembly

**1**. Lay out the blocks and the borders. (Fig 4)
**2**. Sew the centre nine blocks together in rows of three and then join the rows to form the centre nine-patch unit.
**3**. Sew the short border strips to opposite sides of the centre unit.
**4**. Attach the remaining top and bottom borders to the quilt.

## QUILTING AND FINISHING

### Backing

**1**. Cut and join the backing fabric to fit the quilt, overlapping by 2in all the way round. Press any seams open.
**2**. Cut the batting to exactly the same size.

Fig 4

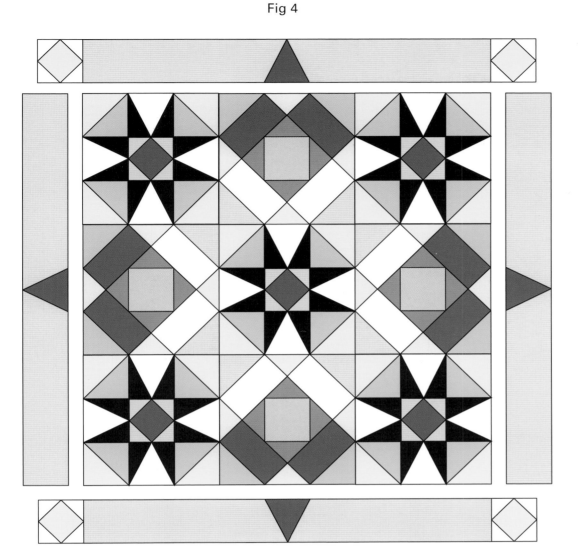

## Quilting

**1**. Make the quilt sandwich of top, batting and backing and secure with safety pins, quilt tacks or basting spray if machine quilting, or by tacking if hand sewing. (See Sewing Basics, page 17.)
**2**. Quilt as desired.

## Binding

**1**. Measure the perimeter of the quilt and join 2½in wide strips of black fabric in a continuous strip to fit. (See page 16 for details on how to make neat joins.)
**2**. Fold in half along the length and iron flat.

**3**. Refer to Sewing Basics, page 18, for details of attaching the binding.

## Label

Make a label for the back, giving details of the name of your quilt, the date you finished it, your name and the town you live in.

## Hanging Sleeve

Refer to Sewing Basics, page 18, for details of attaching a hanging sleeve.

# Turn of the Season

**Above:** 'Turn of the Season' 57in x 70in

All Saints Church is at the heart of the business district and medieval centre of Bristol. There has been a church on this site since the 12th century, and in the Middle Ages the area was home to some of Bristol's wealthiest merchant families, many of which lavished money and attention on the church. The latest changes took place in the mid 19th century when the Victorian tiled floor was laid.

On entering the church two distinct designs meet your eyes. The first, at the western end of the nave, is laid out in an attractive design of multicoloured tiles. The second interesting set of tiles leads up to the altar through the choir and is a riot of white, bright green and encaustic tiles of blue, cream and terracotta, all on point and looking very similar to a 'Log Cabin' design. (See Block Library, page 112.)

Here we have a basic 'Variable Star' that is common to many floors, but this one is delightfully coloured with a central encaustic circular pattern in terracotta on cream. The central units of the block borders, which are inverted 'Flying Geese', are black with pale green triangles and a darker green in the four corners. This block is surrounded by a chocolate brown frame with lighter brown corner squares and is set on point.

What makes this design really stand out is the sashing area, which forms a pretty 'Ohio Star' design. White star points and black triangles surround the central encaustic tile, echoing the centre of the main blocks in cream on terracotta. Since the design is set on point it makes the white stars the principal focus of the pattern. The border in pale brown has pretty floral black and cream encaustic tiles spaced apart at regular intervals that are framed on both sides with strips of chocolate brown. The borders are edged with a further ribbon-like chain of tiny flowers.

**Top:** The nave of All Saints Church
**Above left:** Close-up of the floor tiles
**Left:** A comparable detail of the finished quilt

I started to add to my collection of marbled fabrics to replicate the colours of the tiles as faithfully as I could. I knew that the real challenge would be the encaustic tiles. The search was on to find fabric that would represent the feeling of this intricate pattern. Then I found what I felt could be a good substitute – some brightly coloured orange batik with streaks of red and bubbles of grey and white. These would form the focal point I was looking for. By cutting into particularly highly coloured areas of the fabric, I was able to choose sections that were alike and that would give me the vibrancy I needed to make this quilt come alive. In addition I found a marvellous creamy brown batik fabric streaked in darker brown exactly like marble. By adding some chocolate brown and two shades of marbled green and plain black fabrics I had the palette I was looking for.

**Above left**: 'Turn of the Season' and the nave floor
**Top right**: All Saints Church
**Below right**: Detail of the altar tiles

**Above:** 'Let The Sun Shine'
52½in x 52½in quilted by Tracey Periera

## Variation in Blue and Yellow

I love putting blue and yellow together because it sets up a vibrancy that is both immediate and appealing. For a contemporary version of 'Turn of the Season', I knew that this combination was going to give me the fresh appeal I was looking for. I made just four of the main blocks, giving them deep blue and yellow chequerboard centres that provide texture and vitality. By setting the blocks on point I altered the focus of the nine smaller sashing stars. I gave these wavy stripe centres to echo the centres of the main blocks but at the same time provide a change of rhythm. The royal blue frame makes the centre of the quilt stand out and I echoed this by framing the bright yellow border on both sides to match. The candy-stripe blue and yellow bias binding is inspired by the ribbon borders on the nave floor and completes this sunny quilt.

49

# Turn of the Season

**MATERIALS**

**Fabric**
A variety of 100% cotton fabrics
44in wide in colours to represent
the tiles:
¾ yard red-orange batik
1¾ yards black
½ yard pale green
½ yard dark green
1½ yards chocolate brown
2½ yards dark cream
½ yard white

**Batting**
65in x 78in

**Backing**
4 yards your choice

**Fabric marking pens, light and dark**

## CUTTING *Measurements include ¼in seam allowances*

**Red-orange**
2 strips (4½in wide). Cut into
    12 squares (4½in)
4 strips (2½in wide). Cut into
    64 squares (2½in)

**Black**
9 strips (2½in wide). Cut into
    48 rectangles (2½in x 4½in). The
    remainder is for the binding
2 strips (3¼in wide). Cut into
    20 squares (3¼in)
16 strips (1½in). Cut into 176
    squares (1½in); 8 strips (1½in x
    3½in). The rest is for sashing

**Pale green**
6 strips (2½in wide). Cut into
    96 squares (2½in)

**Dark green**
3 strips (2½in wide). Cut into
    48 squares (2½in)

**Chocolate brown**
16 strips (2½in wide). Cut into
    62 strips (2½in x 10½in)

**Dark cream**
29 strips (2½in wide). Cut into
    88 squares (2½in); 31 strips (2½in
    x 10½in); 100 strips (2½in x 3in);
    44 strips (2½in x 7in)
2 strips (3¼in wide). Cut into
    20 squares (3¼in)

**White**
4 strips (3¼in). Cut into 40
    squares (3¼in)

## BLOCK ASSEMBLY

### Block : 8in square

**1.** To make 'Flying Geese', use a fabric marker pen to draw a diagonal line across the wrong side of all the 2½in pale green squares.
**2.** Take one 2½in x 4½in black rectangle. Place one pale green square on the corner exactly, pin on each side of the marked line and sew on the line. (Fig 1a)
**3.** Trim the spare part of the corner from both fabrics. (Fig 1b)
**4.** Turn back and press the pale green triangle towards the corner. (Fig 1c)
**5.** Repeat on the opposite corner. (Fig 1d)
**6.** Assemble the block with a 4½in red-orange square at the centre and with 2½in dark green squares at the corners. (Fig 1e)
**7.** Make 11 more blocks.

Fig 1a          Fig 1b

Fig 1c          Fig 1d

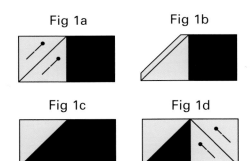

Fig 1e

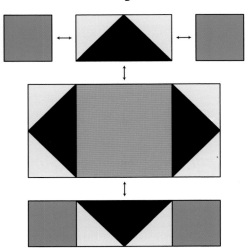

### Block 2: 6in x 10in

**1.** Sew one 2½in x 10½in chocolate brown strip to each long edge of a 2½in x 10½in dark cream strip. (Fig 2)
**2.** Make 31 blocks.

Fig 2

### Block 3: 6in square

**1.** Use a fabric marker pen to draw a diagonal line across the wrong side of all the white and dark cream 3¼in squares.

Fig 3a    Fig 3b

Fig 3c          Fig 3d

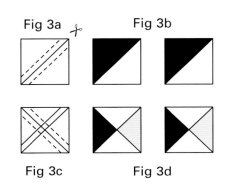

**2.** Place one black and one white 3¼in square right sides together and sew on the light side ¼in from each side of the marked line. (Fig 3a)
**3.** Cut the square in half along the marked line and press open to reveal two squares, half white and half black. (Fig 3b)
**4.** Repeat with the dark cream and white 3¼in squares.
**5.** Draw a line across the diagonal of all these pieces and place one black-and-white and one cream-and-white piece right sides together with the white triangles opposite each other. Sew on the light side ¼in from each side of the marked line. (Fig 3c)
**6.** Cut the square in half along the

Fig 3e

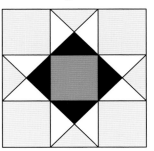

marked line and press open to reveal two pieced squares of four triangles. Use a square ruler to make sure that your block is 2½in square including ¼in seam allowances. (Fig 3d)
**7.** Make 80 of these units altogether.
**8.** Assemble 20 blocks with a 2½in red-orange square at the centre, four 2½in dark cream squares at the corners and four triangle units in between. (Fig 3e)

### Assembling the Inner Quilt

**1.** Lay out all the blocks as shown overleaf. (Fig 4)
**2.** Join the blocks in horizontal rows and then join the rows together. You will find it easier and more accurate to join the rows by pressing one row in one direction and the next row in the opposite direction.

### Block 4: 2in square

**1.** Use a pale fabric marker pen to draw a diagonal line across the wrong side of the 1½in black squares.
**2.** Place a black square exactly at the corner of a 2½in red-orange square and machine along the marked line. Trim off the spare fabric. (Fig 5a overleaf)
**3.** Press back the black triangle towards the corner. Repeat on the opposite corner. (Figs 5b and 5c)
**4.** Repeat on the remaining two corners. (Fig 5d)
**5.** Make 44 blocks altogether.

## Border Strip Sets

1. To make the four corner blocks, cut eight 2½in dark cream squares in half along the diagonal. Sew one triangle to opposite sides of four of the Block 4s.

2. Press outwards and repeat on the remaining opposite sides of the four corner blocks.

3. Square up the four corner blocks to be 3¼in square, including a ¼in seam allowance.

4. Join a 2½in x 3in dark cream strip to opposite sides of one Block 4. (Fig 6a)

5. Press the central block outwards. Make 40 Block 4 strip sets like this.

6. Lay the strips alternately with 2½in x 7in dark cream strips to sew Seminole style. (Fig 6b)

7. Sew two long strips with nine Block 4 sets with an extra dark cream strip at each end. Press back and trim to form a corner, leaving a ¼in seam allowance above the points.

8. Use a light marker pen to draw a line just over ¼in beyond the points of the blocks and cut away the spare triangles each side of the strips to form chevron border strips. (Fig 6c)

9. Join a 1½in x 3½in black strip to two opposite sides of the four corner blocks. (Fig 6d)

10. Sew one corner block to each end of the nine-block chevron strips. (Fig 6e)

11. Sew two long strips with 11 Block 4 strip sets Seminole style as in step 7 above, but this time leave the ends longer.

12. Measure the length of the quilt through the centre and join two 1½in wide black strips. Cut the joined strips to fit the centre length measurement. Make three more strips exactly the same (four in total).

13. Cut the long chevron border strips with 11 blocks to the same

Fig 4

Fig 5a    Fig 5b    Fig 5c    Fig 5d

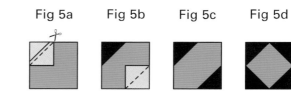

Fig 6a

Fig 6b

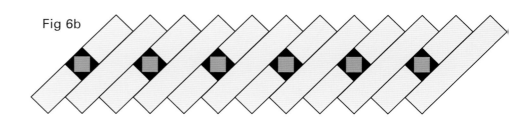

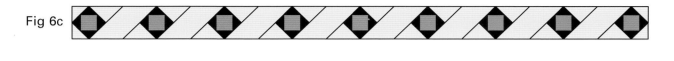

**Fig 6c**

**Fig 6d** 　　　　**Fig 6e**

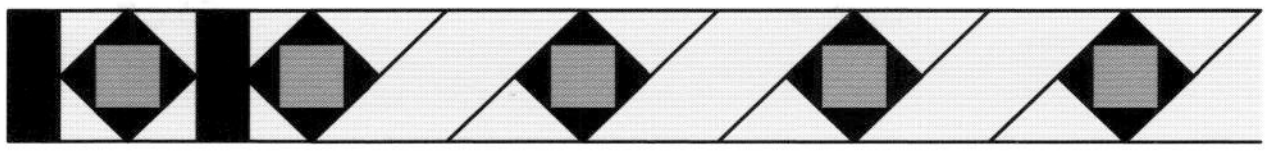

length as the centre length
measurement.

**14.** Sew the long black strips to
each long edge of the two long
chevron border strips.

### Quilt Assembly

**1.** Lay out the blocks and border
strip sets as indicated. (Fig 7)

**2.** Join the two long border strips
to each long edge of the quilt. To
do this accurately, measure the
middle of both the borders and
the sides of the quilt and mark
with a pin. Match the pins and
pin both ends. Pin the rest of the
seam to fit and then carefully
stitch in place.

**3.** Measure the width of the quilt
through the centre. Join two 1½in
wide black strips and trim to fit
the centre width measurement.
Make three more strips exactly
the same and sew them to each
long edge of the top and bottom
chevron border strips.

**4.** Join these top and bottom
borders to the quilt.

### QUILTING AND FINISHING

#### Backing

**1.** Cut and join the backing fabric
to fit the quilt, overlapping by 2in
all the way round. Press any
seams open.

**2.** Cut the batting to exactly the
same size.

#### Quilting

**1.** Make the quilt sandwich of top,
batting and backing, and secure
with safety pins, quilt tacks or
basting spray if machine quilting,

Fig 7

or by tacking if hand sewing. (See
Sewing Basics, page 17.)

**2.** Quilt as desired. I stitched in
the ditch along most of the seams
to stabilize the blocks and then I
stipple quilted the borders. I used
straight lines elsewhere to create
a geometric look.

#### Binding

**1.** Measure the perimeter of the
quilt and join 2½in wide strips of
black fabric in a continuous strip
to fit. This will be the binding.

**2.** Fold in half along the length
and iron flat.

**3.** Refer to Sewing Basics, page
18, for details of attaching the
binding.

#### Label

Make a label for the back, giving
details of the name of your quilt,
the date you finished it, your
name and the town you live in.

#### Hanging Sleeve

Refer to Sewing Basics, page 18,
for details of attaching the
hanging sleeve.

# *Terracotta Flower Garden*

**Above:** 'Terracotta Flower Garden'
34½in x 34½in

The Lake District, with its majestic landscape of lakes and mountains, is a popular holiday destination in Great Britain. Kendal, to the south, is the gateway to the Lakes. From the 14th century it was a centre of the wool trade and it remains a working town with a lively market. Its main attraction for me, however, is its parish church, one of the largest in England, which has five aisles. I was thrilled to find a really unusual tile design at the back of the church surrounding the ancient font.

The floor design around the font includes a large area that looks very much like a series of sunflower heads. The sunflowers comprise black octagons surrounded by cream 'petals'. These are interspersed with small black squares on a background of brown octagons. The curved encaustic tiles of the border design make an attractive edge. It didn't take me long to decide that this particular floor would inspire a quilt.

The octagons plus 'petals' and squares were going to be a challenge to piece and I thought long and hard about how to achieve all those set-in pieces successfully. There are no regular blocks that could be used to make up this pattern without making many seams, which would detract from the design as a whole, so I decided to keep to the original shapes and work out how to piece them. I finally came up with two methods, and by using quite different types of fabrics I realized it would be possible to make two interesting and very distinct quilts (see left and page 57).

**Left**: The tiles in Kendal Parish Church with the finished quilt resting on the font

55

For the original tile design, I employed a technique using fusible web (Bondaweb), which I ironed on to the back of batik fabrics in rich colours as close to the originals as I could find. I cut brown, black and cream fabrics from templates with no seam allowances. Then I used a hot iron to press them on to a background calico, which had first been marked with the entire pattern of the quilt. Once the whole design was in place, I finished it by outlining between the tiles with neat satin stitch to represent the grouting.

Re-creating the border presented a further challenge, but by substituting the curvy encaustic details with a gold-on-black regular diamond motif fabric I was able to enhance the design without losing any of its originality. I completed the narrow cream line between the border and inner tile design with a wide, close satin stitch and echoed that colour in the binding.

**Above** : Kendal Church
**Below left**: The floor tiles and ornate border design
**Below right**: Detail of the central panel of 'Terracotta Flower Garden'

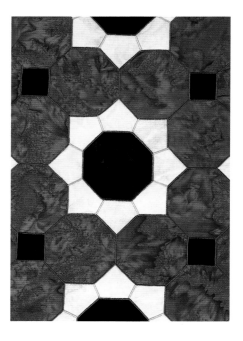

**Above:** 'Mystic Sunflower'
24½in x 24½in

## A Floral Alternative

The obvious way to replicate the design was to piece it by hand over papers – the 'English Paper Piecing' method. I used this method for a contemporary version of this pretty pattern. For this particular quilt, I wanted to use fabrics to represent a vibrant summer version of intricate flower heads and I was lucky enough to find what I wanted from Jason Jenter's line of 'The Butterfly Queen' from In the Beginning Fabrics.

I made plastic templates drafted from the original shapes I had used for the 'Terracotta Flower Garden', but I needed extra templates for the corners and outer centre triangles. First I traced around them on to paper and then I traced them on to the fabrics, adding a ¼in seam allowance. I experimented with the fabric design until I found a shape that I liked that fitted the template. I pieced the inner square by hand, and added the sashing and four corner pieces by machine.

# Terracotta Flower Garden

## QUILT SIZE 34½in x 34½in

## MATERIALS

**Fabric**
A variety of 100% cotton fabrics
44in wide in colours to represent
the tiles:
1 yard brick red
½ yard cream
½ yard black
½ yard black and gold
1½ yards calico

**Binding**
1 yard cream

**Batting**
38in x 38in 100% cotton

**Backing**
2 yards your choice

**Fusible web (Bondaweb)**
4 yards 18in wide

**2 sheets 11in x 8½in template
plastic**

**Blue fabric marker pen**

**Permanent fine black felt-tip pen**

**Large sheet of paper**

**Thread**
1 reel light cream rayon
2 reels dark grey rayon

## MAKING YOUR TEMPLATES

**1.** Place the template plastic over
the printed templates on page 60
and trace using a ruler and the
permanent black felt-tip pen.
Label each template on top with
the appropriate letter.
**2.** Cut all four plastic templates
accurately with paper scissors,
a craft knife or an old rotary
cutting blade.

## CUTTING A

*Cut across the width of the
fabric. Measurements include ¼in
seam allowances*

**Cream**
4 x 2½in strips
**Calico**
40in square as background

## CUTTING B

*Iron fusible web to the back of
the remaining fabrics before
cutting out*

**Brick red**
24 of template A (page 60)
24 of template B (page 60)
**Cream**
72 of template C (page 60)
**Black**
9 of template A (page 60)
16 of template D (page 60)
**Black and gold**
4 strips (3in) giving a central
  pattern as a border

## QUILT ASSEMBLY

Fig 1

### Positioning the Pieces

**1.** Press the calico flat. Fold it in half and then press along the centre fold. Fold in half the other way and press. This will give you guidelines for the placement markings.

**2.** Place your templates on a large piece of white paper and draw round them to make a replica of the basic design. Include one whole flower and the surrounding petals, octagons and squares.

**3.** Mark the design on the calico with a blue marker pen. To do this use a light box or stretch the calico over a window with masking tape. Place the paper under the calico and mark the design on the calico, starting in the centre. Add a 3in border all round, making sure that the corners are square. (Fig 1)

**4.** Place your black and brick red octagons, black squares and cream 'petals' in piles where you can easily reach them.

**5.** Lay the calico over the ironing board with the central folds showing. Heat up your iron.

**6.** Remove the backing paper before placing each piece in its right place on the calico.

**7.** Starting with a black octagon (A), place it so that the edges butt up to the marked lines on the central octagon on the calico. Press it in place.

**8.** Take eight cream 'petals' (C), peel off the backing papers and place them around the black octagon, butting them up exactly to the edge of the octagon and up to the marked design lines on the calico.

**9.** Press them in place too.

**10.** Continue with the surrounding brick red octagons (A) and black squares (D).

**11.** Gradually build up the rest of the pieces, adding them so that they match the marked lines exactly and pressing as you go. Add the edge pieces (B) last.

### Border

**1.** Measure the quilt from top to bottom through the centre. Check that the measurement is the same from side to side, through the centre.

**2.** Trim the four border strips to that measurement plus 8in to allow for pattern matching.

**3.** Peel off the backing paper and place the strips one by one, making sure that the pattern matches in the corners and in the centre of each border and that it is the same along each edge. You may want to cut a 45° mitre at each corner as I did.

**4.** Press the border strips on to the calico, butting up to the outside edge of the quilt.

### Backing

**1.** Cut and join the backing fabric to fit the quilt, overlapping by 2in all the way round. Press any seams open.

**2.** Cut the batting to exactly the same size.

### Quilting

**1.** Make the quilt sandwich of top, batting and backing, and secure with safety pins, quilt tacks or basting spray if machine quilting, or by tacking if hand sewing. (See Sewing Basics, page 17.)

**2.** Make a 10in square sample sandwich with exactly the same fabrics and batting as your quilt, with bonded fabric pressed on to calico, then batting and backing.

3. Select satin stitch on your sewing machine and experiment on your 10in sample with the stitch width and length until you have a stitch that is just wide enough to cover the joins between the pieces. Make sure that the tension is correct and that the lower thread is not visible on the top. (I usually use bobbin thread the same colour as the thread in the top.)

4. Practise stopping and starting and going around the corner of a square. Make sure the thread is secured so that it cannot unravel when you have finished.

5. Use the cream rayon thread to stitch all the joins in between the cream 'petals'.

6. Use the grey rayon thread to stitch all the joins between the red brick octagons.

7. Use the same thread to stitch around all the squares.

8. Return to the 10in sample and adjust your satin stitch to ¼in wide. Experiment until you have a stitch that gives an even coverage. Make sure that the tension is correct and that the lower thread is not visible from the top.

9. Use cream rayon thread and ¼in satin stitch to work along the edges between the octagons and the border.

## Binding

1. Measure the perimeter of the quilt and join 2½in wide strips of cream fabric in a continuous strip to fit. (See page 16.)

2. Fold in half along the length and iron flat.

3. Refer to Sewing Basics, page 18, for details of attaching the binding.

## Label

Make a label for the back, giving details of the name of your quilt, the date you finished it, your name and the town you live in.

## Hanging Sleeve

Refer to Sewing Basics, page 18, for details of attaching the hanging sleeve.

*Templates for 'Terracotta Flower Garden'*
*Shown actual size*

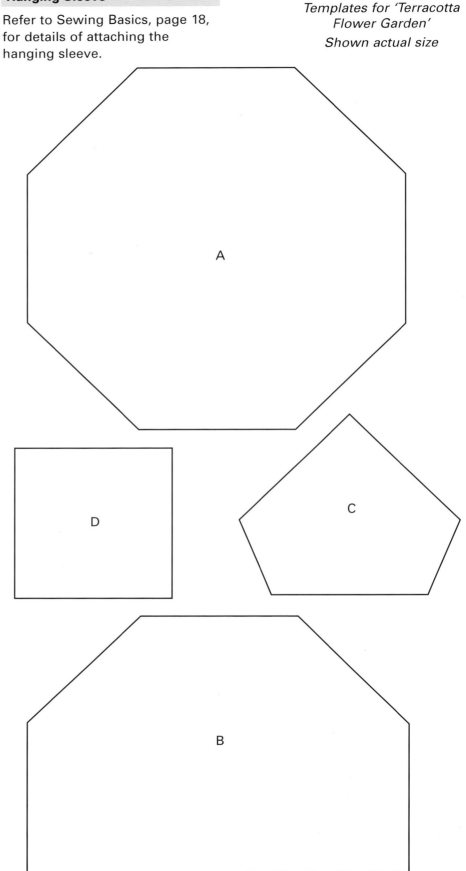

# Mystic Sunflower

## QUILT SIZE: 24½in x 24½in

## MATERIALS

### Fabric
A variety of 100% cotton fabrics 44in wide. I used mostly 'The Butterfly Queen' by Jason Jenter from In the Beginning Fabrics
½ yard orange
½ yard bright red
½ yard light green patterned
⅛ yard bright blue
½ yard dark blue stripe
½ yard dark green stripe

### Binding
¼ yard bright red

### Batting
28in square 100% cotton

### Backing
1 yard your choice

### Template card or plastic

### A4 sheet of 80 gram white paper

### Fabric marker pen

### Permanent fine black felt-tip pen

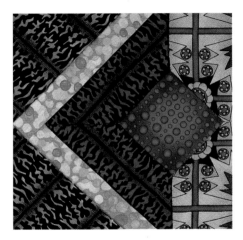

## Cutting *Templates include ¼in seam allowances*

**Orange**
1 of template E (page 63)
4 strips (1⅛in x 18in)
**Bright blue**
8 of template F (page 63)
**Light green patterned**
8 of template E
**Bright red**
4 of template G (page 63)
4 strips (2½in x 30in)
**Dark blue stripe**
4 of template H (page 63)
4 of template H reversed
4 of template J (page 63)
**Dark green stripe**
2 squares (14in)

## Using the Templates

**1.** Place the template plastic over the printed templates and trace around the outside edge using a ruler and the permanent black felt-tip pen. Label each template with the appropriate letter.
**2.** Cut your plastic templates accurately with paper scissors, a craft knife or an old rotary cutting blade.
**3.** Write R on the reverse of template H.
**4.** Cut out all the shapes as instructed left, but experiment first, placing the templates E on the fabric to find a design that links together well and forms a focus for the quilt.
**5.** Now trace all the templates

without the ¼in seam allowance on to white paper. You will need nine of template E, eight of template F, four of templates G and J and eight of template H.

## Quilt Assembly

**1.** Place the template papers on the wrong side of the cut fabric pieces and turn in the ¼in seam allowance. Tack (baste) them down from the back, being careful to fold in at the points for accuracy. (Photo 1)

**2.** Lay out your pieces for the central square following the diagram. (Fig 2)

**3.** Match one edge of the central orange octagon (E) to a blue 'petal' (F) with right sides together. Using matching thread and taking tiny stitches hand sew in place, making sure that the ends match exactly.

**4.** Continue to add the rest of the petals one by one and then sew their sides together to form a flower shape.

**5.** Now sew the green outer ring of octagons (E) to the blue 'petals' and then sew the green sides together. Add the red squares (G) followed by the four dark blue stripe triangles (J) and eight corner pieces (H and HR).

**6.** Remove the papers and press the whole piece carefully from the back and then the front. Make sure the outer pieces now include the ¼in seam allowance for adding the sashing strips.

**7.** Measure across the centre width and trim two orange strips exactly that length. Sew them to the top and bottom by machine and press outwards.

**8.** Measure across the centre width again and trim the two remaining orange strips. Sew them to the two opposite sides and press outwards.

**9.** Cut the two 14in dark green squares in half on the diagonal.

Fig 2

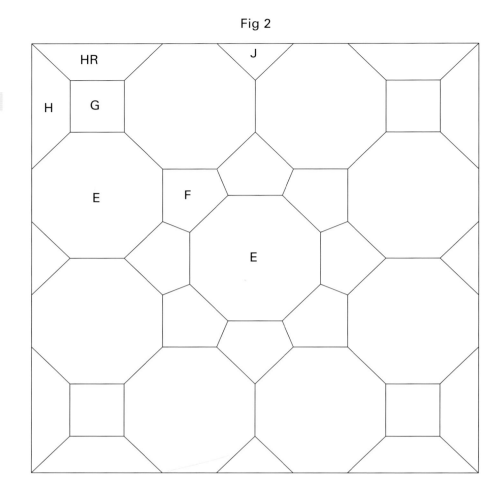

Fold each large triangle in half and mark with a pin.

**10.** Fold the quilt top in half from top to bottom and mark with a pin. Matching the pins, sew a green triangle to the top and bottom of the quilt. Take care not to stretch the bias edge of the dark green fabric. Add the two remaining triangles.

**11.** Use a square ruler to square up the quilt to a size you like, making sure that you have at least ¼in seam allowances for adding the binding.

## Quilting and Finishing

Back, quilt and label the quilt and then add the hanging sleeve in the same way as the 'Terracotta Flower Garden'. (See pages 59–60.)

## Binding

**1.** Measure the perimeter of the quilt and join 2½in wide strips of bright red fabric in a continuous strip to fit. (See page 16.)

**2.** Fold in half along the length and iron flat.

**3.** Refer to Sewing Basics, page 18, for details of attaching the binding.

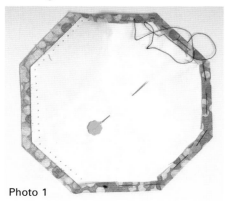

Photo 1

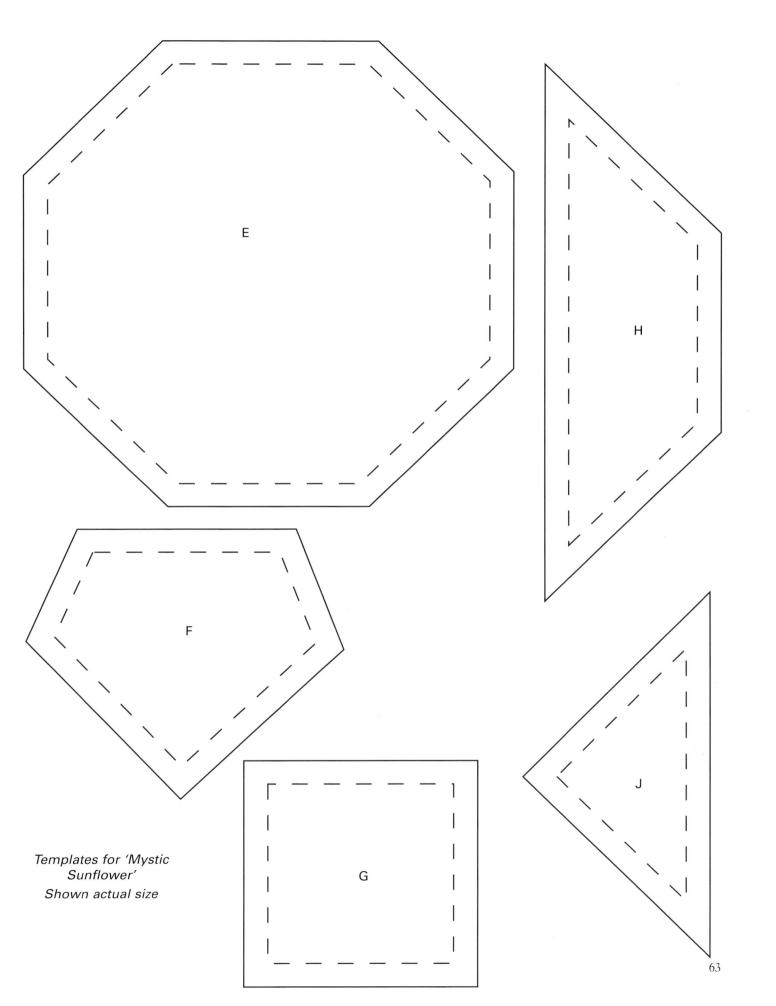

E

H

F

J

G

*Templates for 'Mystic Sunflower'*
*Shown actual size*

63

# Scottish Fantasia

**Above:** 'Scottish Fantasia' 40in x 40in
**Opposite, top:** Central design of St Andrew's Cathedral altar tiles

It was quite by chance that I discovered the tile patterns that inspired this quilt. They were among a riot of different designs in St Andrew's Cathedral in Inverness, Scotland and just cried out to be made. As you can see from the tiles themselves (opposite, top) the pinwheels, with their bright white and rich green triangles, bring your eye to focus on the central circle with its intricate cream pattern overlaid on a further circle of orange with an outer ring of blue. The four less-intricately patterned corner tiles are edged in blue and surrounded by terracotta and four corner cream tiles.

Another feature that drew me to create this particular quilt was the dark brown and green outer zigzag border. This is a traditional border for quilts, though not often used, and here I achieved it by using the Seminole technique (see page 70) outlined in satin stitch. The corner blocks of the whole design are common to many tiled floors and here I have given them bright blue centre squares.

My collection of marbled fabrics came into its own as I gathered together the colours to make this quilt. The central design would not be easy to replicate, but I resolved this by cutting a square in rich blue and overlaying a circle of a distinctive dark orange batik. Finding a fleur-de-lys quilting stencil allowed me to create my own appliqué version of the cream central image on the tiles.

**Far right:** View of the altar floor tiles
**Right:** Detail of a pinwheel in the quilt

St Andrew's Cathedral has an array of fascinating designs, which I found enthralling. While the altar tiles provided the inspiration for the quilt design shown on the previous page, I could have chosen from many more. The scenic centrepiece of the vibrantly coloured circular design (top right) would lend itself to appliqué and possibly foundation paper piecing, while the corner fleur-de-lys could be adapted from the stencil template used in my quilt. The more usual terracotta, cream and black tiles of the aisle leading to the altar (right) are full of potential for the quilter as are the 'Ohio Star' variations of the tiles shown below. The simpler dark brown squares with a white central cross (below right) are enhanced by their border of triangles. (See Block Library, page 112.)

**Top left:** St Andrew's Cathedral
**Top:** Decorative circular centrepiece with corner fleur-de-lys
**Above:** View of the aisle
**Left:** Close-up of the floor tiles, showing Ohio Star variations

**Above:** 'Finding David' 24in x 24in

## 'Finding David' Quilt

For a more contemporary feel, I chose to re-create the altar tiles using brightly coloured fabrics from Africa, which I embellished with Indian mirrors embroidered into circles. The addition of the gold star fabric and the Seminole piecing of the black-and-white stripe edged with green gives this quilt an exuberant feel. These design elements certainly add a sense of fun to the piece and make it look quite different from the original quilt, even though it is exactly the same design.

During our journey to the north of Scotland, I had, quite by chance, met up with a second cousin of mine whom I had not seen since I was 10 years old! I dedicated this small quilt to him and called it 'Finding David'.

# Scottish Fantasia

## MATERIALS

**Fabric**

A variety of 100% cotton fabrics
44in wide in colours to
represent the tiles:
1 yard peach
½ yard cream
¼ yard white
¼ yard vibrant orange
¼ yard dark blue
1½ yards mid green
¼ yard dark green
1 yard mid brown
½ yard dark brown

**Binding**

1 yard mid brown

**Batting**

1½ yards 100% cotton

**Backing**

1½ yards of your choice

**Fusible web (Bondaweb)**

½ yard

**Stitch & Tear or Sulky Solvy**

## CUTTING *Measurements include ¼in seam allowances*

**Peach**

2 strips (2½in wide). Cut into
16 rectangles (2½in x 4½in)
8 squares (4⅞in). Cut in half
diagonally
4 squares (3¾in). Cut in half
diagonally

**Cream**

1 strip (2½in wide). Cut into
32 squares
4 squares (4½in)
1 square (8½in)
4 squares (2⅞in). Cut in half
diagonally

**White**

8 squares (3¾in). Cut in half
diagonally

**Vibrant orange**

4 squares (4½in)
1 square (6in)

**Dark blue**

4 squares (4½in)
1 square (8½in)
4 squares (3¾in). Cut in half
diagonally

**Mid green**

8 strips (1⅞in wide)
16 squares (2½in)

**Dark green**

4 squares (3¾in). Cut in half
diagonally

**Mid brown**

4 strips (1⅞in wide)
4 squares (3¾in). Cut in half
diagonally
4 strips (2½in wide) for binding

**Dark brown**

12 squares (2⅞in). Cut in half
diagonally
8 strips (24¾in x 2½in)

## BLOCK ASSEMBLY

### Block 1: 8in square

**1.** Join a dark blue triangle to each small peach triangle. Make into a square by joining on a large peach triangle. (Fig 1a)
**2.** Make up the block by adding two of these squares to one 4½in cream square and one 4½in vibrant orange square. (Fig1b)
**3.** Make four blocks.

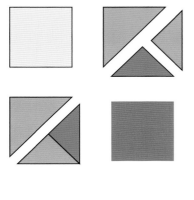

Fig 1a

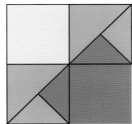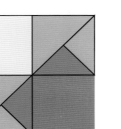

Fig 1b

Fig 2a

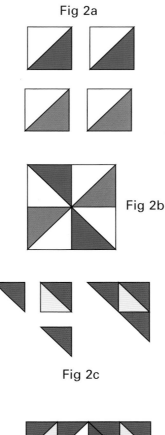

Fig 2b

Fig 2c

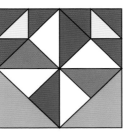

Fig 2d

**6.** Satin stitch around the orange circle with matching thread. It helps to put some support underneath to add stability, such as Sulky Solvy or Stitch & Tear.
**7.** Place the stencil centrally over the blue square and fuse. (Fig 3d)
**8.** Satin stitch around the stencil with matching thread using either Sulky Solvy or Stitch & Tear.

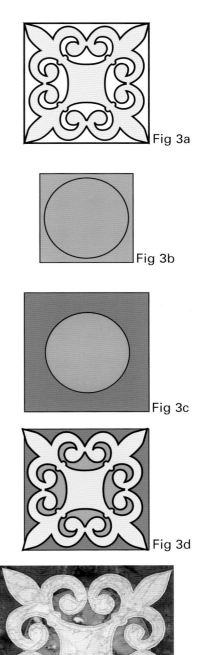

Fig 3a

Fig 3b

Fig 3c

Fig 3d

### Block 2: 8in square

**1.** Join a dark green triangle to a white triangle to make a square. Repeat. Join the mid brown and white triangles to make two squares in the same way. (Fig 2a)
**2.** Join them together to make a pinwheel as illustrated. (Fig 2b)
**3.** Join the 2⅞in cream and dark brown triangles to form two units, as shown. (Fig 2c)
**4.** Add two 3¾in peach triangles to adjacent sides of the pinwheel.
**5.** Add two brown and cream triangle units to the remaining sides of the pinwheel. (Fig 2d)
**6.** Make four blocks.

### Block 3: 8in square

**1.** From the Bondaweb, cut one 8½in square and one 6in square.
**2.** Trace the decorative template on page 71 and enlarge.
**3.** Trace it on to the back of the 8½in square of web and then fuse it to the 8½in cream square. Cut out the design. (Fig 3a)
**4.** Trace a 5½in circle on to the 6in square of web and fuse it to the 6in orange square. (Fig 3b)
**5.** Cut out the circle and fuse it to the centre of the 8½in dark blue square. (To find the centre, fold the square into four and place the circle centrally.) (Fig 3c)

## Block 4: 8in square

**1.** Place a 2½ in cream square on one corner of each peach rectangle. Machine from corner to corner across it. Cut the surplus ¼in from the stitch line. (Fig 4a)

**2.** Fold back the cream square and press. (Fig 4b)

**3.** Repeat on the opposite corner. (Fig 4c)

**4.** Make four identical units.

**5.** Lay out the units, the 2½in mid green squares and the 4½in blue square as shown in the diagram and sew together in rows. (Fig 4d)

**6.** Finally sew the rows together to make the block. (Fig 4e)

**7.** Make four blocks.

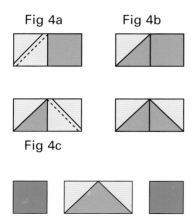

Fig 4a  Fig 4b

Fig 4c

Fig 4d

Fig 4e

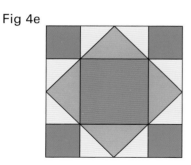

## Strip Set

**1.** Join three 1⅞in strips in the following order: mid green, mid brown, mid green, making sure they are staggered as indicated. (Fig 5a)

**2.** Repeat as above but stagger the strips in the opposite direction. (Fig 5b)

**3.** Cut the strips at an angle of 45° and 2½in apart, making six pieces in each direction as indicated.

**4.** Sew the pieces together to form a long strip with six chevron units. (Fig 5c)

**5.** Place a ruler just over ¼in along the outer edges of the brown chevrons and draw a line. This will be your cutting line.

**6.** Cut along both lines. (Fig 5d)

**7.** Make four strip sets.

**8.** Sew a dark brown strip to each long edge, matching and pinning the ends and the centre first, before sewing.

**9.** Make a total of four units.

Fig 5a

Fig 5b

Fig 5c

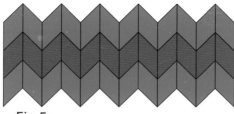

Fig 5d

## Quilt Assembly (opposite)

**1.** Lay out the blocks and the chevron strip sets as indicated. (Fig 6a)

**2.** Sew the centre nine blocks together in rows of three and then join the rows to form the centre nine patch.

**3.** Sew a chevron strip set to each side of the centre nine patch.

**4.** Sew a Block 4 to each end of the remaining chevron strip sets.

**5.** Attach one to the top and one to the bottom of the quilt. (Fig 6b)

## Quilting and Finishing

### Backing

**1.** Cut and join the backing fabric to fit the quilt, overlapping by 2in all the way round. Press any seams open.

**2.** Cut the batting to exactly the same size.

### Quilting

**1.** Make the quilt sandwich of top, batting and backing, and secure with safety pins, quilt tacks or basting spray if machine quilting, or by tacking if hand sewing. (See Sewing Basics, page 17).

**2.** Quilt as desired. I stitched in the ditch along most of the seams to stabilize the blocks and worked minimal decorative quilting, as I felt the design spoke for itself.

### Binding

**1.** Measure the perimeter of the quilt. Take the 2½in wide strips of mid brown fabric and join them in a continuous strip. (See page 16.)

**2.** Fold in half along the length and iron flat.

**3.** Refer to Sewing Basics, page 18, for details of attaching the binding.

Fig 6a

Fig 6b

**Label**

Make a label for the back, giving details of the name of your quilt, the date you finished it, your name and the town you live in.

**Hanging Sleeve**

Refer to Sewing Basics, page 18, for details of attaching the hanging sleeve.

*Block 3 appliqué template – enlarge on a photocopier by 141%*

# Chinese Lanterns

The east end of Bristol Cathedral was originally an Augustinian monastery and parts of the building go back to the 12th century. The floors would have been plain flagstones, but in the second half of the 19th century the size of the building was more than doubled to form the present-day cathedral. As part of the transformation a fine new floor was laid, covering the whole of the choir and sanctuary. Unlike many other tiled floors laid at this time, the area in front of the altar and along the choir stalls is made up of marble tiles of great intricacy. They are full of vibrant colour, very similar to the original Cosmati floors to be found in Italy and elsewhere in mainland Europe.

The central medallion of Mariner's Compasses is surrounded by a variety of shapes and patterns that include 'Square Within a Square', diamonds and triangles in many sizes. The most fascinating part of these complex patterns is that as the design increases or diminishes in size, so the shapes around it change in perspective and become longer or shorter. It is a true tour de force.

**Left:** 'Chinese Lanterns' 79in x 38in

The whole floor is a riot of colour — white veined marble forms the background to bright reds, many shades of green and grey, ochres, yellows and black. My first impression was that this entire floor was so complicated that I could not re-create it. Yet on subsequent visits I realized that sections of it could be isolated and were in fact made up of easily recognizable traditional patchwork patterns. I only needed to make decisions about which parts to use as my inspiration for a series of quilts.

One design that particularly caught my eye, immediately to the right and left of the central medallion, was a tile design that reminded me of Chinese Lanterns. It was geometric, simple and rather plain in comparison to its surrounding patterns, yet I found it really effective and appealing. Once I had drafted the basic shapes of a diamond and a rectangle, the design was easily achieved and that also meant that it would be very simple to piece.

**Top**: The Mariner's Compasses
**Left**: The section of floor that caught my eye
**Above**: Detail of the finished quilt

73

Now to choose the fabrics that would represent this colourful floor. It would add interest to making a floor-tile quilt if I were to use colours other than terracotta, black, brown and cream. The Free Spirit Fabric Company from New York generously supplied the major part of the fabric for this quilt in the exact colours I needed from their 'Color Connector' range.

Once the diamonds were pieced, I couched a thick black thread along all the dividing lines between the diamonds to mimic the lines on the actual floor. Then I fused on the rectangles at the diamond intersections, which were finished with satin stitch.

**Top left**: Bristol Cathedral
**Top right**: Detail of a tile border

**Below**: Close-up of the Mariner's Compasses

**Above:** 'Woodrow Victoriana Tea Cups' 53in x 42½in

## Moving On

Wanting to take the diamond idea further, I had fun trying out various designs. I was inspired not only by the cathedral floor tiles, but also by some quilts I had seen in California made by Ann Ito. As I developed the design further I worked together with Creative Grids (UK) Ltd to produce a special acrylic diamond template made with holes for marking fabric and designed to split the shape asymmetrically into four. Once the pieces were cut, I turned them upside down and joined them into diagonal strips. I was pleased that the resulting quilt was far removed from the original floor that had given me the jumping off point for my design. Woodrow Studios generously provided the fabric for this quilt.

# Chinese Lanterns

## QUILT SIZE 79in x 38in

### MATERIALS

**Fabric**
A variety of 100% cotton fabrics 44in wide in colours to represent the tiles:
2 yards pale turquoise
½ yard pale yellow
1 yard gold
½ yard beige grey
½ yard light grey
1 yard mottled grey
1 yard black
½ yard red

**Batting**
86in x 45in of your choice

**Backing**
2½ yards of your choice

**Fusible web (Bondaweb)**
1½ yards (18in wide)

**Permanent fine black felt-tip pen**

**Fabric marking pen or pencil**

**Diamond Template (Creative Grids (UK) Ltd) or template plastic**

**Extra rulers**
15½in square acrylic ruler
12½in x 6½in acrylic ruler

**Thread:**
Pale grey for piecing
Black rayon
Red rayon
Thick black for couching

## CUTTING A *Measurements include ¼in seam allowances*

Use the Creative Grids Diamond Template or template A (page 78).

**Pale turquoise**
29 diamonds (A)

**Pale yellow**
5 diamonds (A)

**Gold**
13 diamonds (A)

**Beige grey**
6 diamonds (A)

**Light grey**
6 diamonds (A)

**Mottled grey**
4 strips (6½in wide)

**Black**
6 strips (2½in wide) for binding

## CUTTING B *Iron fusible web to the back of the remaining black and red fabrics before cutting out*

**Black**
2 strips (3in wide). Cut 19 of template B; 4 of template C; 6 of template D (page 78)

**Red**
2 strips (3 in wide). Cut 19 of template B; 4 of template C; 6 of template D

## QUILT ASSEMBLY

**1.** Lay out the diamonds using the photograph of the quilt as a colour guide. (Fig 1a)

**2.** Sew the diamonds together in rows diagonally. Press the seams in alternate directions on each row. (Fig1b)

**3.** Sew the rows together, butting up the joining seams and making sure that they match exactly.

**4.** Lay the square ruler on each corner, giving just over ¼in seam allowance over the edge of the diamonds and cut the corners. (Photo 1c)

**5.** Place the 12½in x 6½in ruler across the edge of the remaining four sides, making sure you leave just over ¼in seam allowance. Cut along the edge of the quilt from corner to corner. (Photo 1d)

**6.** To stop the sides from stretching use a larger stitch than you use for piecing to sew a line of stay stitching just ⅛in from the edge all around the edge of the quilt.

### Border

**1.** Join the 6½in mottled grey border strips into a continuous strip. (See Sewing Basics, page 16.) Press the seams open.

**2.** Measure the quilt through the centre from top to bottom. Cut two of the mottled grey border strips the length of the quilt plus 14in.

**3.** Fold each strip in half and mark the centre with a pin. Measure half the length either side of the pin and mark with pins.

**4.** Fold the quilt top in half and mark with a pin.

**5.** Matching the centre pins and the ends of the quilt with the outside pins on the border, closely pin a border strip to each side of the quilt. You may have to ease slightly at this point.

**6.** Sew each border from end to

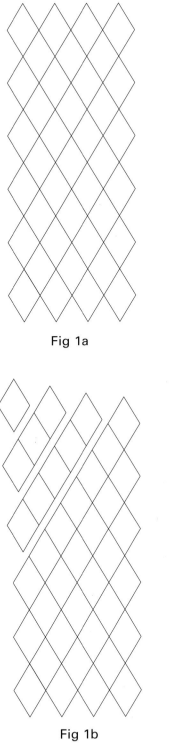

Fig 1a

Fig 1b

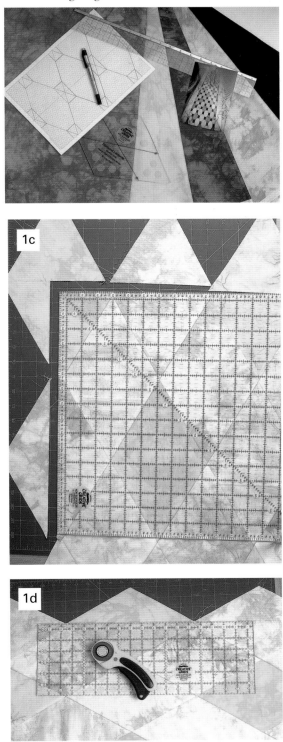

1c

1d

end, leaving the extra fabric at the ends for mitring the corners. Press the border to the outside.

**7.** Measure across the centre of the quilt from side to side and cut two more border strips the width of the quilt plus 14in.

**8.** Attach one to the top and one to the bottom of the quilt in the same way as the side borders. (Fig 2 overleaf)

**9.** Mitre the corners of the borders. (See Sewing Basics, page 17.)

## Couching

1. Cut and join the backing fabric to fit the quilt, overlapping by 2in all the way round. Press any seams open.
2. Cut the batting to match.
3. Make the quilt sandwich of top, batting and backing, and secure with safety pins, quilt tacks or basting spray if machine quilting, or by tacking if hand sewing. (See Sewing Basics, page 17.) If using tacks or pins, do not put any on the lines between the diamonds.
4. Make a practice quilt sandwich using exactly the same fabric, batting and backing as in the quilt. Use black rayon on the top and practice couching the thick black thread with a very narrow zigzag stitch so that you can hardly see the stitching.
5. Return to the quilt and stitch along all the diagonal lines between the diamonds, couching the black thread. Secure the threads at the ends of the rows with a backstitch or a 'fix' stitch if your sewing machine has one.

### Small Rectangles

1. Peel off the back of the fusible web (Bondaweb) and place the full black rectangles (B) one by one in rows, as indicated in the main photograph of the quilt. Press gently with a warm iron to fuse in place.
2. Repeat with the red rectangles (B).
3. Continue with the remaining top and bottom black and red pieces (C).
4. Finally, press and fuse the remaining side pieces (D) in place on the quilt.
5. Fuse a piece of Bondaweb to a 3in x 2in piece of spare fabric and fuse on to your practice sample. Use black rayon to practice until you have a tiny satin stitch that covers the edge of the fused piece neatly.

6. Working diagonally across the quilt, satin stitch all the edges of the black fused rectangles. I found it easier to sew from top right to bottom right and then from left to right of the rectangles in rows down the quilt. (Fig 3a)
7. Repeat on the opposite sides of the rectangles. (Fig. 3b)
8. Complete the top, bottom and side fused pieces. Secure the stitch at the beginning and end of the satin stitch line.
9. Now use red rayon thread to stitch the red rectangles as above.
10. Finally, couch black thread around the quilt between the centre pattern and the border. Secure the stitching with a backstitch or a 'fix' stitch if your sewing machine has one.

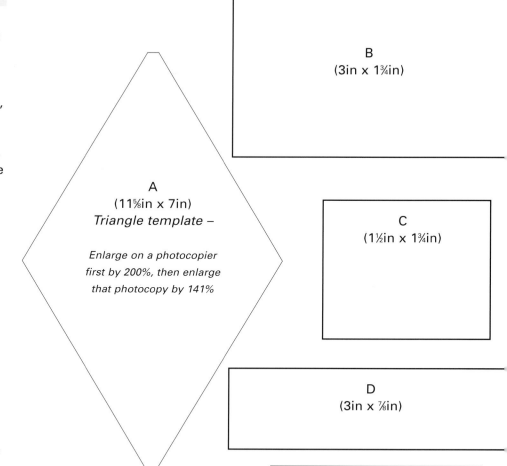

A
(11⅝in x 7in)
*Triangle template –*

*Enlarge on a photocopier first by 200%, then enlarge that photocopy by 141%*

B
(3in x 1¾in)

C
(1½in x 1¾in)

D
(3in x ⅞in)

Fig 2

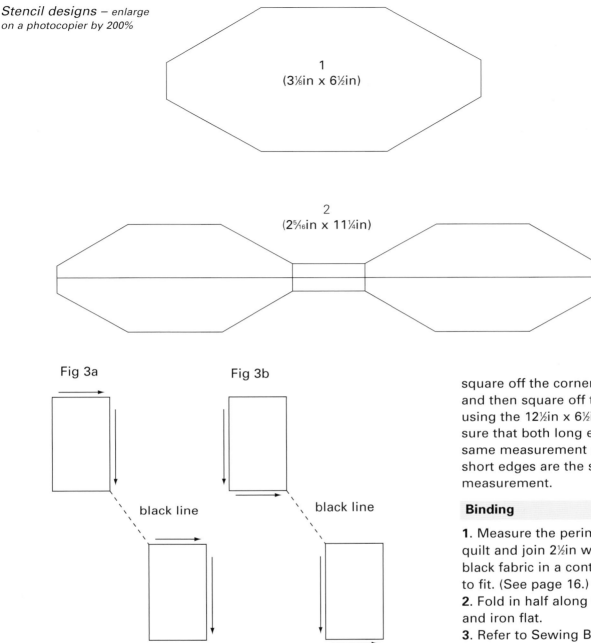

Stencil designs – *enlarge on a photocopier by 200%*

1
(3⅛in x 6½in)

2
(2⁵⁄₁₆in x 11¼in)

Fig 3a

Fig 3b

black line

black line

## QUILTING AND FINISHING

### Quilting

**1**. Using the template plastic and the felt-tip pen, trace and cut out the quilting stencils 1 and 2.
**2**. Stencil 1 is a cut-off diamond shape that I designed to quilt in every diamond. Use matching thread. For ease of quilting, use the same method as for attaching the rectangles so that you quilt diagonally down the quilt on one side of the shapes, then down the other side.
**3**. Stencil 2 is made up of smaller diamonds and rectangles. Starting at the corners, mark the border until you are close to the centre, then make the final central long motif fit between the two ends. Quilt around the border stencil design.
**4**. Stipple around the border stencil to the edge of the quilt.
**5**. Use the 15½in square ruler to square off the corners of the quilt, and then square off the edges using the 12½in x 6½in ruler. Make sure that both long edges are the same measurement and that both short edges are the same measurement.

### Binding

**1**. Measure the perimeter of the quilt and join 2½in wide strips of black fabric in a continuous strip to fit. (See page 16.)
**2**. Fold in half along the length and iron flat.
**3**. Refer to Sewing Basics, page 18, for details of attaching the binding.

### Label

Make a label for the back, giving details of the name of your quilt, the date you finished it, your name and the town you live in.

### Hanging Sleeve

Refer to Sewing Basics, page 18, for details of attaching the hanging sleeve.

# *Turning the Corner*

**Above:** 'Turning the Corner'
55½in x 66½in

You never know where you are going to find tiles, so it is important always to keep a small camera handy just in case you unexpectedly stumble across a new design. While my husband and I were on holiday in our favourite part of Britain, the Lake District, we had to buy a new toothbrush and were thrilled to discover in a chemist's shop in Ambleside, a superb tiled floor with a pattern that was completely new to me. Permission to photograph was given by the rather bemused owner who became intrigued when I explained that I would make a quilt or two inspired by the tiles on his floor.

The interior design of the floor comprises a series of lines that cross over each other diagonally to form large terracotta Xs. At the intersections between the crosses are smaller crosses in beige with a central green-and-white 'Square Within a Square' block. Beneath this grid is another running vertically and horizontally, which gives an almost three-dimensional feel, as though you are looking down over a series of geometric grids. The background grid is made up of beige rectangles and black triangles with a cream background. Wide chocolate brown sashing frames this central part of the design.

When I came to study the photographs of the border, I realized that as the shop had been so full of shelves and sales stands we had not been able to make a record of how to turn the corner!

**Top left**: View of the Lake District
**Top right**: Ambleside chemist's shop
**Left**: Close-up of the floor tiles
**Below**: Detail of the quilt border

The part of the border that I could see was made of 'Square Within a Square' blocks of green and white, similar to the crossover blocks of the top grid. These were set on point with terracotta and cream triangles. I spent many hours working out the logistics of turning the corner and I am happy with the design I arrived at.

Finding fabrics almost identical to the colours on the floor is always a challenge. If you cannot find the fabric you want at your local quilt shop or at a quilt show, try the Internet or mailing small samples of the colour to shops. One of these methods usually brings success.

While in the Lake District we visited Rydal Church, which was the regular place of worship for the poet William Wordsworth. There I was happy to find an almost identical border design surrounding a charming tile pattern that covered the whole floor of the sanctuary.

**Top left**: The tile border in Ambleside chemist's shop
**Top right**: Corresponding detail of the finished quilt
**Left**: Rydal Church floor

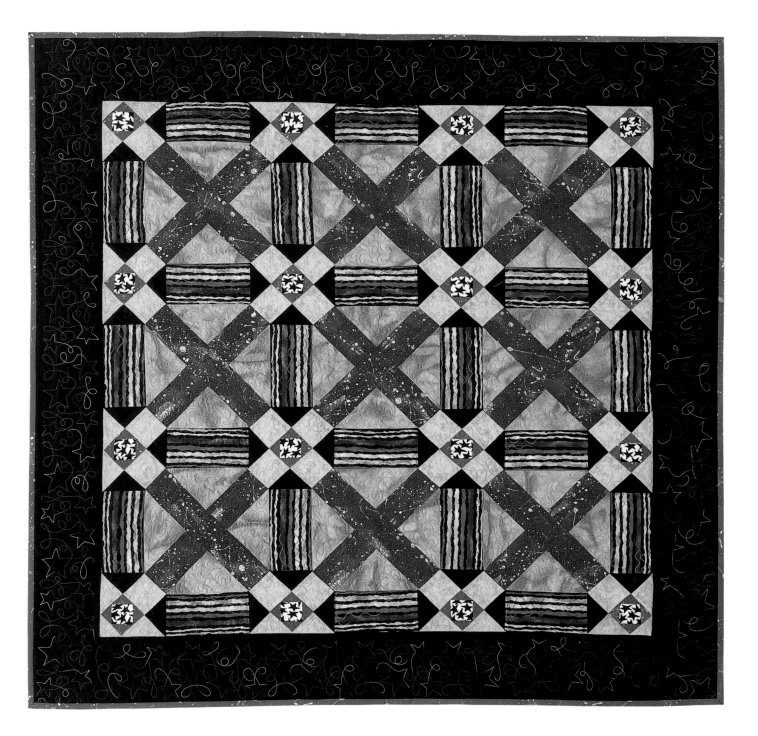

**Above:** 'Stripy Hugs & Kisses'
45½in x 45½in quilted by Jenny Spencer

## Fabric Inspirations

I love collecting fabrics of all kinds, and find that sometimes they inspire me just as much as the floor-tile designs. Some blue, red, lime green and bright yellow 'paint spattered' fabrics cried out to be sewn together with the fabulous wobbly stripe fabric. Using the blue for the long crosses gives this piece a completely different look to the quilt made in the original tile colours. Notice how the black triangles emphasize the crosses of brilliant yellow at the intersections while the black-and-white star fabric adds an extra twist in the red centres. The stars are echoed in the quilting design of the border, added with a variegated primary coloured thread.

# Turning the Corner

## QUILT SIZE 55½in x 66½in

## MATERIALS

**Fabric**
A variety of 100% cotton fabrics
44in wide in colours to represent
the tiles:
1½ yards light brown
1½ yards cream
½ yard black
1 yard dark brown
2 yards brick red
½ yard green
¾ yard white

**Batting**
60in x 70in of your choice

**Backing**
4 yards of your choice

**Fabric marker pen**

**Extra rulers**
Square: 4½in and 6½in

## CUTTING *Measurements include ¼in seam allowances*

**Light brown**
4 strips (3⅜in wide). Cut into
   31 rectangles (3⅜in x 6⅛in)
5 strips (2½in wide). Cut into
   80 squares (2½in)
6 strips (3in wide). Cut into
   72 squares (3in)

**Cream**
3 strips (5in wide). Cut into
   24 squares (5in)
5 strips (3in wide). Cut into
   64 squares (3in)
1 strip (4in wide). Cut into
   8 squares (4in)

**Black**
3 strips (3in wide). Cut into
   31 squares (3in)

**Dark brown**
5 strips (2¼in wide)
7 strips (1¾in wide)

**Brick red**
16 strips (2½in wide). Cut into
   24 rectangles (4½ x 2½in);
   12 rectangles (10½ x 2½in);
   64 squares (2½in). The
   remainder is for the binding

**Green**
4 strips (2½in wide). Cut into
   56 squares (2½in)

**White**
3 strips (1½in wide). Cut into
   80 squares (1½in)
5 strips (2¼in wide). Cut into
   72 squares (2¼in)

## BLOCK ASSEMBLY

### Block 1: 6in square

1. Cut the 3in black squares in half diagonally to make 62 triangles.
2. Sew a black triangle to each end of each 3⅜in x 6⅛in light brown rectangle. (Fig 1a)
3. Cut the 5in cream squares in half diagonally to make 48 triangles.
4. Sew a cream triangle to each long edge of one light brown strip and press. (Fig 1b)
5. Use a 6½in square ruler to square up the block to 6½in, including a ¼in seam allowance all the way round. Make 17 full blocks and 14 with a cream triangle on one side only. (Fig 1c)

### Sashing Strips

1. Sew a 2½in light brown square to one end of a 4½in x 2½in brick red rectangle; press. (Fig 2a)
2. Make 24 of these.
3. Sew a 2½in light brown square to each end of a 10½in x 2½in brick red rectangle; press. (Fig 2b)
4. Make 12 of these.

### Block 2: 2in square

1. Use a fabric marker pen to draw a diagonal line across the wrong side of all the 1½in white squares.
2. Place a white square on the left-hand corner of a 2½in green square and machine stitch from corner to corner along the marked line. (Fig 3a)
3. Cut the surplus ¼in from the stitch line. (Fig 3b)
4. Fold back the white fabric and press. (Fig 3c)
5. Repeat on the opposite corner and then the remaining two corners. (Fig 3d)
6. Make 20 of these 'Square Within a Square' blocks.

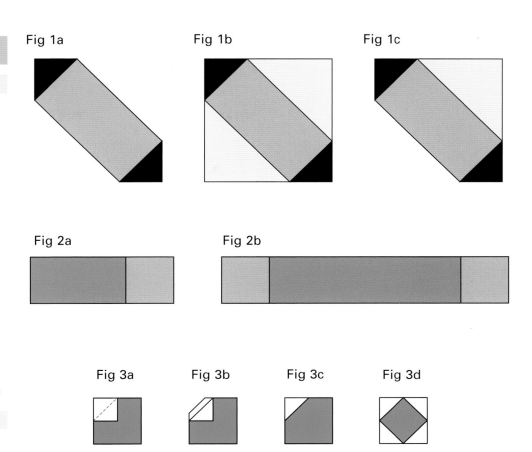

Fig 1a  Fig 1b  Fig 1c

Fig 2a  Fig 2b

Fig 3a  Fig 3b  Fig 3c  Fig 3d

### Quilt Assembly

1. Lay out the blocks and sashing strips as shown in the diagram overleaf. Add light brown squares to the outer green-and-white 'Square Within a Square' blocks as shown. Note that the 10½in x 2½in brick red strips all run diagonally from top left to bottom right. (Fig 4 overleaf)
2. Join the rows together as indicated in the diagram and press well.
3. Using a large square ruler, square up the corners and use a long ruler to trim the edges, leaving just over ¼in seam allowance all the way round.

### Border Block 1: 4in

1. Cut the 2¼in white squares in half diagonally to make 144 triangles.
2. Sew a white triangle to one side of a 2½in green square and press outwards. (Fig 5a, shown on page 87)
3. Repeat on the opposite side. (Fig 5b)
4. Repeat on the remaining two sides. (Fig 5c)
5. Cut the 3in light brown squares in half diagonally to make 144 triangles.
6. Sew on the light brown triangles following steps 1-4 above. (Fig 5d)
7. Use a 4½in square ruler to square up the block, leaving a ¼in seam allowance all the way round.
8. Make 36 blocks.
9. Cut the 4in cream squares in half diagonally to make 16 triangles.
10. Sew a cream triangle to two adjacent sides of one block.
11. Make eight units like this. These will be the border end pieces.

Fig 4

the sides of the quilt. Press outwards. (Fig 7c)

**7.** Measure the width of the quilt across the centre and cut two dark brown strips that length. Sew them to the top and bottom of the quilt. Press outwards.

**8.** Attach a border strip to each side of the quilt and press outwards.

**9.** Sew the two remaining border strips to the top and bottom of the quilt.

## QUILTING AND FINISHING

### Backing

**1.** Cut and join the backing fabric to fit the quilt, overlapping by 2in all the way round. Press any seams open.

**2.** Cut the batting to exactly the same size.

### Quilting

**1.** Make the quilt sandwich of top, batting and backing, and secure with safety pins, quilt tacks or basting spray if machine quilting, or by tacking if hand sewing. (See Sewing Basics, page 17.)

**2.** Quilt as desired. This quilt was stitched in the ditch along most of the seams to stabilize the blocks with minimal decorative quilting because I felt the design spoke for itself.

### Binding

**1.** Measure the perimeter of the quilt and join 2½in wide strips of brick red fabric in a continuous strip to fit.

**2.** Fold in half along the length and iron flat.

**3.** Refer to Sewing Basics, page 18, for details of attaching the binding.

### Border Block 2

**1.** Cut the 3in cream squares in half across the diagonal to make 128 triangles.

**2.** Sew a cream triangle to two adjacent sides of a 2½in brick red square. (Fig 6)

**3.** Make 64 of these blocks.

### Border Assembly

**1.** Sew a Border Block 2 to opposite sides of one Border Block 1. (Fig 7a)

**2.** Make 28 units.

**3.** Join seven units together. Add a Border Block 2 to two border end piece and then attach them, one at each end of your seven-unit strip. (Fig 7b)

**4.** Make four border strips.

**5.** Join the 2¼in wide dark brown strips to make a continuous piece. (See Sewing Basics, page 16.)

**6.** Measure the length of the quilt from top to bottom through the centre and cut two dark brown strips that length.  Sew them to

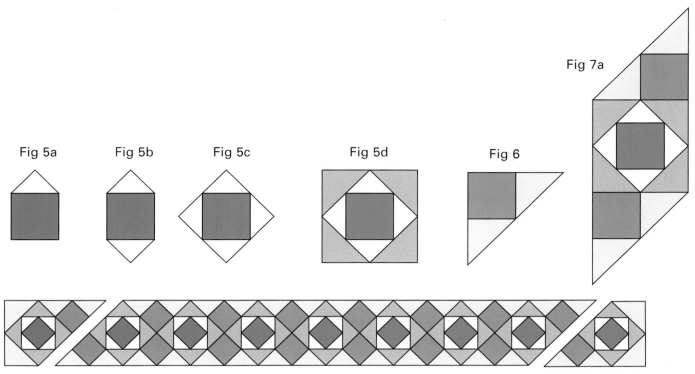

Fig 5a

Fig 5b

Fig 5c

Fig 5d

Fig 6

Fig 7a

Fig 7b

## Label

Make a label for the back, giving details of the name of your quilt, the date you finished it, your name and the town you live in.

## Label

Make a label for the back, giving details of the name of your quilt, the date you finished it, your name and the town you live in.

## Hanging Sleeve

Refer to Sewing Basics, page 18, for details of attaching the hanging sleeve.

Fig 7c

 # Lightning Strike

**Left:** 'Lightning Strike' 60in x 40in

The sanctuary and high altar of Bristol Cathedral were restored at the end of the 19th century and the floor was the subject of massive change. The floor is now an intricate, enormously decorative and highly coloured mosaic. Between the sanctuary and the choir stalls is an area that is less colourful, but nonetheless designed in several attractive patterns. The one that appealed to me most was the border zigzag. (See Chinese Lanterns, page 72, for another quilt based on the tiles in this ancient cathedral.)

The zigzag has long been a traditional setting for the strippy quilt and I often look for this at quilt shows but seldom find it, either as a strippy or as a border. The geometry of the design on this floor is pleasing and I also felt that the colours had an extremely modern look. Indeed when I made the quilt I was struck by the strong lines and in particular the two wide pink and black stripes that gave the quilt a powerful feel. I pieced the quilt exactly as the floor had been laid, with the zigzags made up of individual triangles.

While quilting the zigzag strips, I chose to outline them in straight lines, which further adds to the geometry of the piece. I found the ideal stencil for the rest of the quilt in Shauna Thompson's *Distinctive Designs in Continuous Line*, which I further adapted to fit the triangles.

**Left**: Close-up of the floor tiles
**Below left**: Detail of 'Lightning Strike'
**Below**: The original floor of the cathedral by the choir stalls

**Left:** Bristol Cathedral
**Below:** Comparable details of the tiles and finished quilt

**Right** 'Lightning Strike 2'
40in x 40in
**Far right:** 'Autumnal
Directions' 50in x 40in

## Two Alternative Designs

I made two contemporary versions based on the 'Lightning Strike' design that incorporate the zigzag. The first, 'Autumnal Directions', was made entirely with plaids and stripes and pieces of my husband's old shirt (I told him it was old). I pieced it in half-square triangles using dark and light plus medium and light fabrics for contrast. The appliquéd border adds a folksy note to the quilt.

In my second variation, 'Lightning Strike 2', I highlighted a single zigzag row as a border. This time I made it in vibrant colours but pieced it as the original floor was laid, demonstrating how versatile this design is.

# Lightning Strike

## MATERIALS

**Fabric**
A variety of 100% cotton fabrics
44in wide in colours to represent
the tiles:
2 yards black
2 yards pink
1¾ yards grey
¼ yard yellow

**Batting**
68in x 48in 100% cotton

**Backing**
2½ yards your choice

**1 sheet clear template plastic**

**Permanent fine black felt-tip pen**

## CUTTING *Measurements include ¼in seam allowances*

**Black**
7 squares (11¼in). Cut in half
  diagonally
2 strips (5½in wide)
6 squares (5½in)
5 strips (2½in wide) for binding

**Pink**
13 squares (11¼in). Cut in half
  diagonally
2 strips (5½in wide)

**Grey**
14 squares (11¼in). Cut in half
  diagonally
6 squares (4½in). Cut in half
  diagonally

**Yellow**
6 squares (4½in). Cut in half
  diagonally

## BLOCK ASSEMBLY

### Block 1

**1.** Place the long diagonal side of a yellow triangle right sides together with the edge of a 5½in black square. To do this accurately, fold the triangle in half and mark the centre with a pin. Fold the black square in half and mark it with a pin. Match up the pins and sew along the seam.

**2.** Press outwards and repeat on the opposite side. Press outwards. (Fig 1a)

**3.** Attach two more yellow triangles to the remaining sides using the same method. (Fig 1b)

**4.** Repeat to make two more yellow-and-black blocks and three grey-and-black blocks. Square up all the blocks to 7⅜in, making sure you have a ¼in seam allowance beyond the points all the way round.

**5.** Referring to the diagram, add one large black and one pink triangle to opposite sides of the blocks. (Fig 1c)

**6.** For the top and bottom blocks (one yellow-and-black block and one grey-and-black block), add an extra triangle as shown. (Fig 1d)

**7.** Join the row of blocks to form a strip. (Fig 1e)

### Zigzag Side Strips

**1.** Join grey and black 11¼in triangles together to make a strip the same length as Block 1. Repeat to make a strip of grey and pink 11¼in triangles. (Fig 2a)

**2.** Sew a grey-and-black strip to the black side of Block 1, matching the centres. (I marked the centre of each triangle with a fabric marker, then matched and pinned the marks for accuracy.)

**3.** Sew a grey-and-pink strip to the opposite side of Block 1 in the same way.

Fig 1e

Fig 2a

Fig 1a

Fig 1b

Fig 1c

Fig 1d

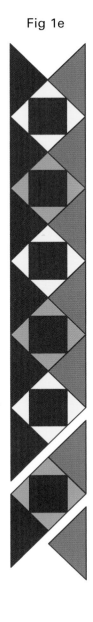

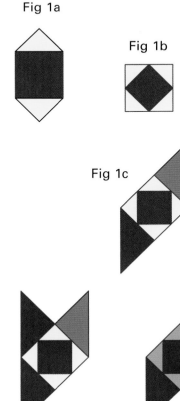

**4.** Cut the waste from the top and bottom of the long strip, making sure that you leave just over ¼in seam allowance beyond the points. (Fig 2b)

**5.** Stay stitch all the way round so that the bias edges will not stretch.

**6.** Join together two more grey-and-pink zigzag strips, referring to the finished quilt for placement.

### Quilt Assembly

**1.** Join the two 5½in strips of black fabric together to make a continuous strip. (See Sewing Basics, page 16.)

**2.** Repeat with the two 5½in strips of pink fabric.

**3.** Measure the length of the central strip with blocks through the centre. Check this measurement on the outside edges – they should be the same.

**4.** Trim both the black and pink 5½in wide strips to this length.

**5.** Assemble the quilt as shown below. (Fig 3)

### QUILTING AND FINISHING

#### Backing

**1.** Cut and join the backing fabric to fit the quilt, overlapping by 2in all the way round. Press any seams open.

**2.** Cut the batting to exactly the same size.

#### Quilting

**1.** Make the quilt sandwich of top, batting and backing, and secure with safety pins, quilt tacks or basting spray if machine quilting, or by tacking if hand sewing. (See Sewing Basics, page 17.)

**2.** Quilt as desired. I adapted a design from Shauna Thompson's

Fig 2b

Fig 3

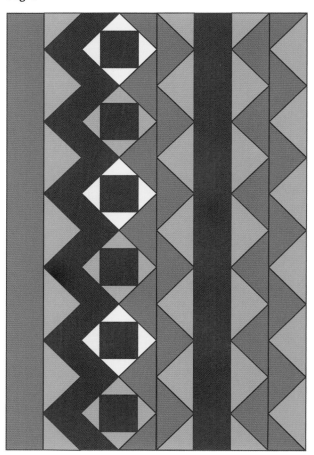

*Distinctive Designs in Continuous Line* and traced it on to template plastic. I used a single motif on the black inner squares and on the black and the pink long strips (Template A). I used the triangular motif in the two outer grey triangle strips (Template B). I stipple quilted the remainder.

### Binding

**1.** Measure the perimeter of the quilt and join 2½in wide strips of black fabric in a continuous strip to fit.
**2.** Fold in half along the length and iron flat.
**3.** Refer to Sewing Basics, page 18, for details of attaching the binding.

### Label

Make a label for the back, giving details of the name of your quilt, the date you finished it, your name and the town you live in.

### Hanging Sleeve

Refer to Sewing Basics, page 18, for details of attaching the hanging sleeve.

Quilting Templates

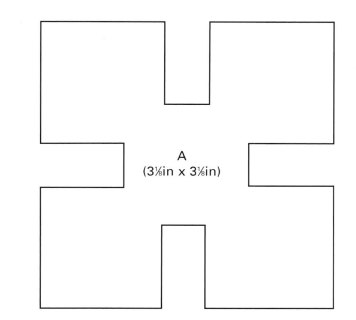

A
(3⅛in x 3⅛in)

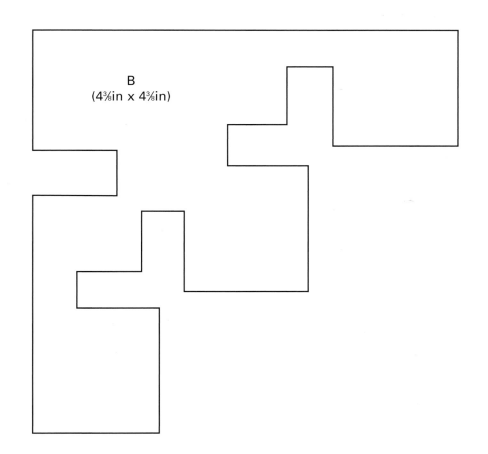

B
(4⅜in x 4⅜in)

# Venetian Celebration

**Above:** 'Venetian Celebration'
104in x 104in

Crossing the lagoon to Venice by boat as the sun sets over the city has to be one of the most magical journeys in the world. To greet you at the eastern end of a vast piazza by the water's edge stands one of the most entrancing buildings in the world, Basilica di San Marco. Known to English speakers as St Mark's, this architectural gem was begun in 830CE and it is thought that the tile patterns date back to the 11th century. Even today, you can stand on over 3,000 square yards of precious 'tesserae', as the tile is called, in glittering colours, rich in symbolism. Many of the designs are of great complexity, laid by artisans working in such valuable materials as lapis lazuli and malachite. For the quilter who is inspired by floor-tile designs, this is the equivalent of being in floor-tile paradise.

It is essential to take a camera and a sketchbook to record the myriad of designs that lie beneath your feet – a true feast for the eyes. Inside and also around the outside of the Basilica there are borders, medallions, rectangles and many other shapes of various colourings. Some of the designs are simple, using four-patch and 'Square Within a Square' and other traditional block patterns, while you can also see vast areas of complex shapes based on divisions of a circle (see below left, for example). Each division is filled with regular shapes, such as triangles, that diminish in size as they near the centre.

**Above**: The tiles that inspired this quilt
**Bottom left**: Divisions of a circle in St Mark's Cathedral
**Bottom right**: Another of the many floor-tile design in St Mark's Cathedral, this one in the shape of a medallion

Left: St Mark's
Cathedral, Venice
**Centre left**: Detail
of the centre
panel
**Bottom left**: The
quilt's corner
design
**Below**: Detail of
the quilt's 'Attic
Window' border

Several designs in this great cathedral inspired me, especially the medallion squares, each one with a different centre. The area of floor tile that I chose to re-create for this book has at the centre a two-row 12-pointed 'Mariner's Compass' in brown and gold, set in a white square on point with black triangles to emphasize the corners. This is surrounded first with inset multicoloured diamond rectangles arranged around red and white 'Squares Within Squares'. The outer border is wide and made up of two components – half-square triangles and 'Attic Windows', both of which have further sashing separations with square corner posts. Each area is divided by a wide white marble sashing strip that also forms the border. Finding the fabrics to make this quilt was part of the fun and I ended up scouring both the UK and the USA for the correct colours. Hobbs Heirloom Fusible batting was generously donated by Creative Grids (UK) Ltd.

Above: 'Klee's Compass'

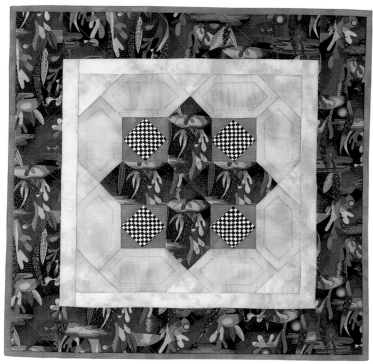

Above: 'From the Forest Floor'

Above: 'Summer Skies'

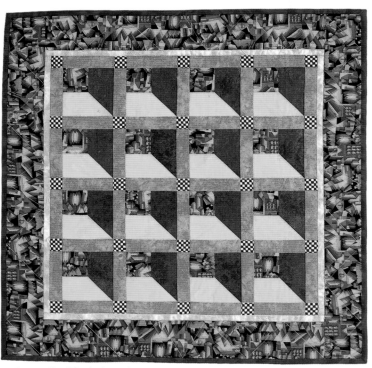

Above: 'In Klee's Attic'

## Contemporary Variations

The quilt I made in the original tile colours is very large and assembled from four component parts, so I decided to make four small contemporary wall hangings to demonstrate the various techniques used to create the original quilt. Fabric from the 'Inspired by Paul Klee' range from Woodrow Studios of London was generously donated for this chapter. I used the bright geometric designs from this fabric range as focus fabrics and added plainer fabrics to emphasize the three-dimensional aspects of the quilts. I used a small black-and-white chequerboard as a common denominator in each of the four quilts and added yellow, orange, green and blue to enhance and enrich the patterns. Techniques used include foundation piecing and setting-in.

# Venetian Celebration

## MATERIALS

**Fabric**
A variety of 100% cotton fabrics 44in wide:

### 'IN KLEE'S ATTIC'
½ yard focus fabric
¼ yard orange
⅛ yard chequerboard
¼ yard royal blue
¼ yard yellow
⅛ yard pale green

### 'SUMMER SKIES'
¾ yard focus fabric
¼ yard pale blue
½ yard bright green
¼ yard orange
¼ yard chequerboard
⅛ yard royal blue

### 'KLEE'S COMPASS'
½ yard focus fabric
¼ yard pale blue
¾ yard orange
⅛ yard chequerboard
¾ yard royal blue

### 'FROM THE FOREST FLOOR'
½ yard focus fabric
⅛ yard orange
⅛ yard chequerboard
¼ yard yellow
¼ yard pale green

**Batting**
For each quilt 1 square (32in)

**Backing**
For each quilt 1 yard your choice

**5in square of freezer paper**

**Template card or plastic**

**Rotary ruler (optional)**

**Fabric marker pen**

## CUTTING *Measurements include ¼in seam allowances*

### 'IN KLEE'S ATTIC'
**Focus fabric**
1 strip (2½in wide). Cut into 16 squares (2½in)
3 strips (3½in wide)
**Orange**
5 strips (1½in wide). Cut into 40 rectangles (1½in x 4½in)
**Black-and-white chequerboard**
1 strip (1½in wide). Cut into 25 squares (1½in)
**Royal blue**
5 strips (2½in wide). Cut into 16 rectangles (2½in x 4⅞in). The remainder is for binding
**Yellow**
2 strips (2½in wide). Cut into 16 rectangles (2½in x 4⅞in)
**Pale green**
2 strips (1in wide)

### 'SUMMER SKIES'
**Focus fabric**
1 strip (5¼in wide). Cut into 4 squares (5¼in)
3 strips (3½in wide)
**Pale blue**
1 strip (5¼in wide). Cut into 4 squares (5¼in)
**Bright green**
1 strip (5¼in wide). Cut into 4 squares (5¼in)
3 strips (2½in wide) for binding
**Orange**
1 strip (5¼in wide). Cut into 4 squares (5¼in)
2 strips (1in wide)
**Black-and-white chequerboard**
5 strips (1½in wide). Cut into 40 strips (1½in x 4½in)
**Royal blue**
1 strip (1½in wide). Cut into 25 squares (1½in)

### 'KLEE'S COMPASS'
**Focus fabric**
1 strip (6in wide)
1 strip (5in wide)
2 strips (2½in wide)
**Pale blue**
1 strip (4in wide)
**Orange**
1 strip (6in wide)
1 strip (5in wide)
3 strips (3½in wide)
**Black-and-white chequerboard**
2 strips (1in wide)
**Royal blue**
1 square (20½in)

### 'FROM THE FOREST FLOOR'
**Focus fabric**
1 strip (4in wide)
3 strips (3½in wide)
**Orange**
4 strips (2½in wide). Cut into 8 squares (2½in). The remainder is for binding
**Black-and-white chequerboard**
1 strip (2½in wide). Cut into 4 squares (2½in)
**Yellow**
1 strip (4in wide)
**Pale green**
2 squares (3in)
2 squares (3¾in)
2 strips (1½in wide)

# 'In Klee's Attic'

## QUILT SIZE: 28½in x 28½in

### Centre Block: 4in

**1.** Matching one end and one side, sew a royal blue rectangle to one side of each focus fabric square, stopping ¼in from the end. (Photo 1a)

**2.** Sew a yellow rectangle to the adjacent side of the focus fabric, stopping ¼in from the end. (Photo 1b)

**3.** Placing the royal blue and yellow rectangles right sides together, draw a line at 45° from the previous seam. Sew to the edge. (Photo 1c)

**4.** Trim off the excess fabric and press the seam open. (Photo 1d)

**5.** Trim the block so that it measures 4½in square. Make 16 of these blocks.

### Quilt Assembly

**1.** Lay out the blocks, orange strips and chequerboard squares as shown in the photograph above. Stitch together in rows, pressing each row in opposite directions. Join the rows.

**2.** Complete the quilt following steps 4–8 for 'Summer Skies', using pale green sashing strips, focus fabric border strips and royal blue binding.

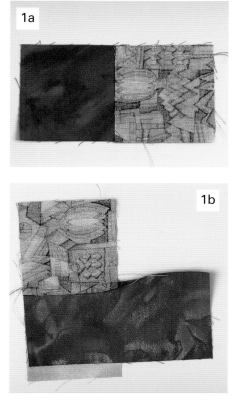

1a

1b

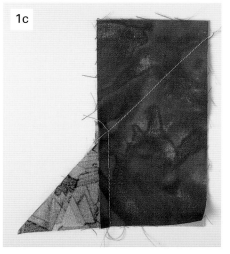

1c

1d

# 'Summer Skies'

## QUILT SIZE: 28½in x 28½in

### Centre Block: 4in

**1.** Each of the pale blue, bright green, orange and focus fabric squares need to be cut into four triangles. First cut across the diagonal once then, without moving the squares, cut them across the opposite diagonal.

**2.** Join the pale blue and orange triangles together in pairs. Join the focus fabric and bright green triangles in the same way.

**3.** Join the two sets together into squares, making sure that the seams match exactly in the centre. Press to one side. Trim to make an exact 4½in square, leaving a ¼in seam allowance all round. Make 16 blocks. (Fig 2)

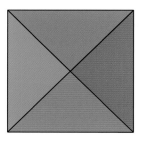

Fig 2

## Quilt Assembly

1. Lay out the blocks, chequerboard strips and royal blue squares as shown in the photograph. Note that I turned one block – according to the Amish quilters, only God is perfect and they always make a deliberate mistake.
2. Join together in rows, pressing each row in opposite directions.
3. Join the rows together.
4. Measure the length down the centre and cut two 1in orange sashing strips that same measurement. Sew one to each side of the quilt. Press outwards.
5. Measure the width across the centre, including the orange sashing strips, and cut two 1in orange strips that length. Sew to the top and bottom of the quilt. Press outwards.
6. Repeat steps 4 and 5 to add the focus fabric border strips.
7. Refer to Sewing Basics, page 17, for making the quilt sandwich. Quilt as desired.
8. Join the 2½in bright green strips to make a continuous strip just slightly longer than the perimeter of the quilt as binding. Add the binding (see Sewing Basics, page 18).

# 'Klee's Compass'

## QUILT SIZE: 23in x 23in

### Mariner's Compass

1. Enlarge the diagram. Most of the circle will fit on to A3 paper (11½in x 16½in). (Fig 3)
2. Make eight photocopies. Cut out 12 identical sections facing one way (A, B and C), including a good ¼in seam allowance. Then repeat for 12 identical sections facing in the opposite direction, (AR, BR and CR).
3. To make templates for cutting the pieces, trace around each of the three sections on to template plastic, leaving a ⅜in allowance all the way round each piece. Place a coloured dot on the top of the templates. Write the letter 'R' for 'Reverse' on the back.
4. Cut out 12 pieces each of A (focus fabric), B (orange) and C (pale blue) with the coloured dot facing on top of the template.
5. Referring to the photographs on page 103, use the lines on the paper as sewing guides and pin the orange piece (B) on to the reverse of the paper, holding it up to the light to check that the seam allowance is covered. (Photo 3a)
6. Place the focus fabric (A), right sides together as shown and use a small stitch on the machine to sew from the back along the black line. (Photo 3b)
7. Trim the seam allowance, leaving about ⅛in. Press towards the edge. (Photo 3c)
8. Add the pale blue pieces (C) as shown. Trim the seam allowance and press. (Photos 3d and 3e)
9. Turn each section over and trim, preferably with a rotary ruler, leaving a ¼in seam allowance all the way round. Make twelve sections (A, B, C). (Photos 3f and 3g)

A   AR

B   BR

C   CR

Fig 3

Enlarge by 328%

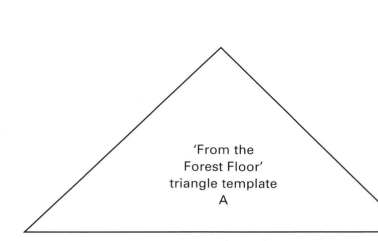

'From the
Forest Floor'
triangle template
A

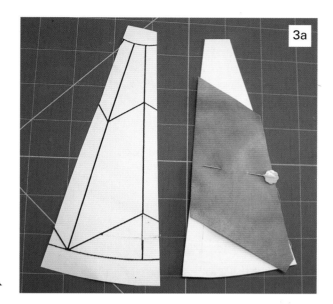

3a

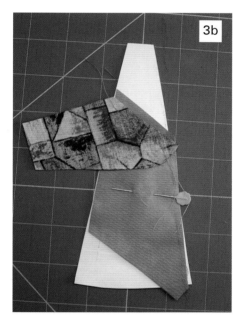

3b

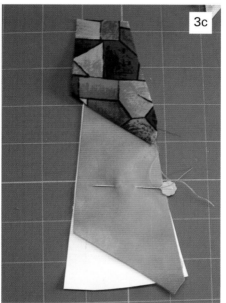

3c

3d

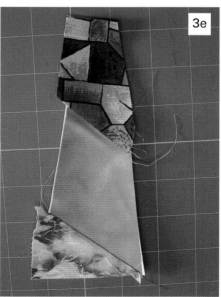

3e

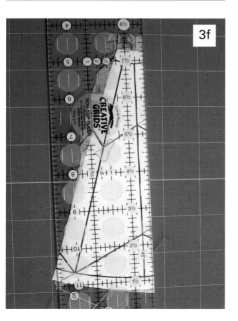

3f

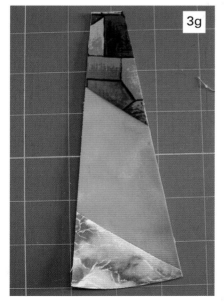

3g

**10.** Repeat for the remaining twelve sections (AR, BR, CR), using the reverse side of the templates. This time cut AR in orange and BR in focus fabric.

**11.** Lay out the sections in a circle and join them together in pairs, then join the pairs to form the compass. Press the seams open.

**12.** Carefully remove the paper and press again.

**13.** Sew a line of stay stitching just ⅛in from the outer edge of the compass. Turn in the outer edge by just under ¼in and tack (baste) it with small stitches.

## Quilt Assembly

**1.** Press the 20½in royal blue square in half and then in half again the other way, so that you are able to find the centre.

**2.** Place the compass carefully on top of the square, matching a point to each fold. Pin all the way round and appliqué in place, either by hand or machine. (I used invisible thread). Press.

**3.** Trace the centre circle from a photocopy on to the matt side of the freezer paper and cut out.

**4.** Press the freezer paper, shiny side down on to the back of the pale blue fabric and cut round it, adding an extra-bare ¼in seam allowance.

**5.** Remove the freezer paper and place it matt side down on the back of the fabric. Carefully press the fabric seam allowance on to the shiny side.

**6.** Pin the pale blue circle in the centre of the compass and appliqué as before.

**7.** From the back, slit the centre of the royal blue square and remove the freezer paper.

**8.** Complete the quilt following steps 4–8 for 'Summer Skies' (see page 102), using chequerboard sashing, an orange border and focus fabric binding.

# 'From the Forest Floor'

## QUILT SIZE:: 23in x 23in

## 'Square Within a Square' Block: 4in

**1.** Cut the 2½in orange squares in half across the diagonal to make 16 triangles.

**2.** Sew an orange triangle on to one side of a 2½in chequerboard fabric square and press outwards. (Fig 4a)

**3.** Repeat on the opposite side and then on the remaining two sides. (Figs 4b and 4c)

**4.** Make four blocks.

## Quilt Assembly

**1.** Cut a 5½in x 2¾in rectangle of template plastic. Trace the triangle template A, on page 103, on to paper and use it to trim two opposite ends of the rectangle to produce a lozenge shape (4d).

**2.** From the 4in yellow strip cut eight lozenges and from the 4in focus fabric strip cut four lozenges. Mark a dot ¼in from the long edges on the wrong side of the fabric using a fabric marker pen. (Fig 4d)

**3.** Cut the 3in and 3¾in pale green squares in half diagonally.

**4.** Lay out all the pieces as in the finished quilt.

**5.** Join a yellow lozenge to each orange and chequerboard square, sewing between the dots – i.e. ¼in from the edge. Join pairs with a focus fabric lozenge. (Fig 4e)

**6.** Sew a small pale green triangle to one top and one bottom yellow lozenge. (Fig 4e)

**7.** Sew these strips to the inner focus fabric lozenges.

**8.** Sew a small pale green triangle to one yellow lozenge from each side edge, and then sew them to the central piece.

**9.** Sew the large pale green triangles to the corners.

**10.** Add the pale green sashing, focus fabric border and orange binding as in steps 4–8 of 'Summer Skies' (see page 102).

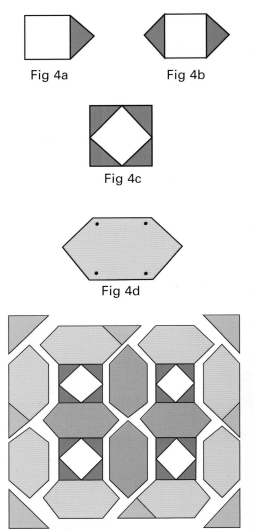

Fig 4a    Fig 4b

Fig 4c

Fig 4d

Fig 4e

# Gallery

This section displays a range of wonderful quilts, all inspired by tiles, which are made by a number of different quilt artists. I hope they will inspire you with their gorgeous colour combinations and imaginative designs to make your own quilts based on tiles. All works are copyright in the name of the artist.

## 'Opus Sectile 2'

Janet Cook

**Size:** 40in x 63in

Photograph by
Neil Porter

This is Janet's second quilt
based on the Great
Pavement in Westminster
Abbey, which dates back
to 1269. Richard Foster's
book, *Patterns of Thought*,
shows a watercolour from
the Abbey's collection,
which inspired 'Opus'.
Janet was moved when
she first saw this
incredibly beautiful floor,
with its elegant geometry
and its enigmatic message
hidden in the inscription.
Her quilt was made with
fabrics as close as possible
to the original colours
and shapes and her aim
was for it to be
mysterious and timeless,
like its source.
(Shown sideways.)

## 'Marbled Stars'

Judy Mathieson

**Size**: 47in x 52in

Photograph by Jack Mathieson

'Marbled Stars' was inspired by a floor in Bristol Cathedral. It is a simplified version of an earlier quilt called 'Bristol Stars' (see page 11) and instead of eight stars around an inner star, 'Marbled Stars' has six circling stars. Much of the fabric in the quilt was hand marbled by textile artist Marjorie Bevis of Oakland, Oregon USA.

# 'Mosaic Stars'

Anne Ohlenschlager

**Size:** 88in x 77in

Photograph by Neil Porter

This quilt was inspired by the floor of St Maria Maggiore in Rome. It was pieced and quilted entirely by machine and is made up of many different grey, white and black tonal fabrics, including some silver lamé. The six dark pink silk triangles lift the monochrome of the quilt.

# 'Venezia'

Gisela Thwaites

**Size:** 76in x 76in

Photograph by Neil Porter

This quilt is based on a floor mosaic at the entrance to St Mark's Cathedral in Venice, and Gisela has stayed true to the colours of the mosaic. The quilting pattern in the centre and the four 'triangles' of the quilt are adaptations of the wrought-iron windows in St Mark's. This quilt was hand pieced and quilted.

# 'Renovation'

Jennifer Stokes

**Size:** 102in x 102in

Photograph by Michael Wykes

'Renovation' is based on a tiled floor in Jennifer's house, which is undergoing complete renovation. In the top-left portion of the quilt Jennifer shows the original floor pattern while the modern replacement is shown bottom right. In the centre Jennifer cleverly represents the way the old tiles have broken or are being removed, ready for replacement. This quilt was machine pieced and quilted.

# 'Coriolis'

Judy Dales

**Size:** 58in x 69in

Photograph by Photo House Inc.

Judy works mainly with curved lines in her quilts but she has always loved the precision and intricacy of geometric patterns and she is especially drawn to designs based on a circular grid. Although this quilt represents part of an Italian tile design from the 13th century, Judy was also inspired by a folk art design painted on a Costa Rican wagon wheel. The geometry depends on the equal division of a circle and a precise grid of lines, which together create a feeling of movement. (Shown sideways.)

# Block Library

There are many different blocks used in floor-tile designs. This is a small selection for you to use as a resource. Divided into families of 9 and 16-patch blocks and borders, you can draft them yourself either on graph paper or with computer software. By making multiple copies of each block, you can arrange them as you wish. Combining two different blocks in the same family can produce intriguing secondary designs. Colour them in as you wish to find your unique floor-tile quilt.

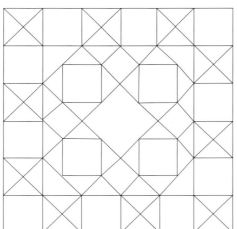

**Inverness Cathedral 1 – expanded 9- patch block**

# Nine-patch Blocks

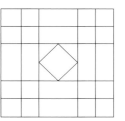

Gatcombe Manor

Jackfield Museum 1

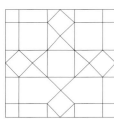

Inverness Cathedral 2

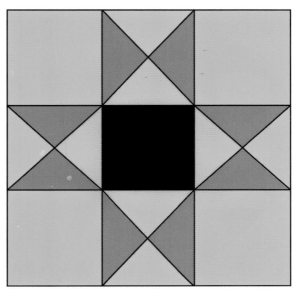

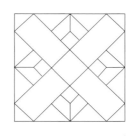

Clifton Club

# Sixteen-patch Blocks

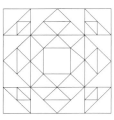 Jackfield Museum 2

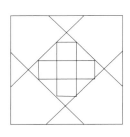 Jackfield Museum 3

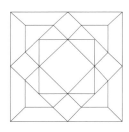 Jackfield Museum 4

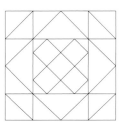 Inverness Cathedral 3

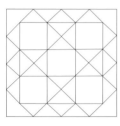

Inverness Cathedral 4

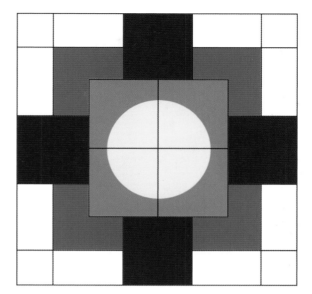

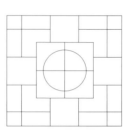

All Saints, Bristol

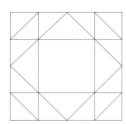

St Stephen's Church
Font 1

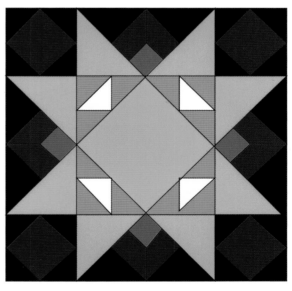

St Stephen's Church
Font 2

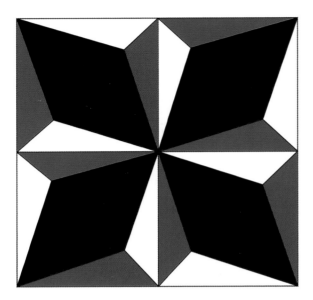
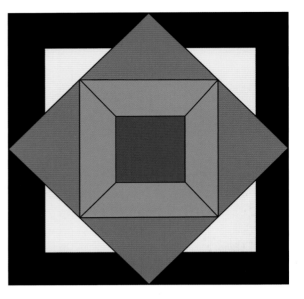

Collioure Church, France

Jackfield Museum 5

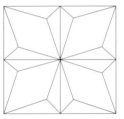
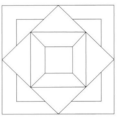

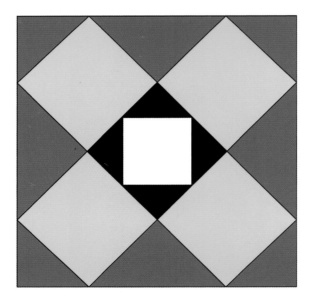
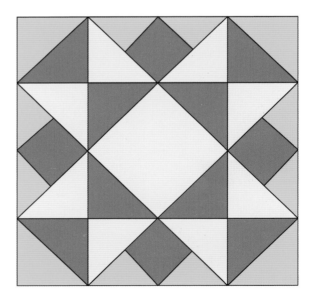

Robin's Hallway

Jackfield Museum 6

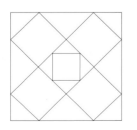
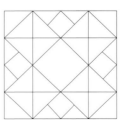

# *Borders*

Bristol Cathedral 1

Bristol Cathedral 2

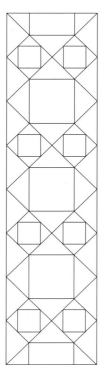

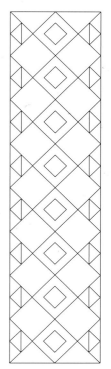

## Bristol Cathedral 3

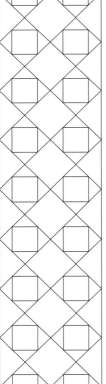

## Dartmoor Church

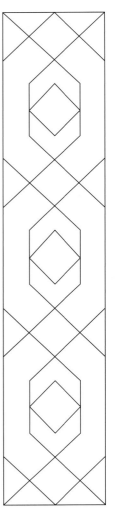

## St Stephen's Church 1

## St Stephen's Church 2

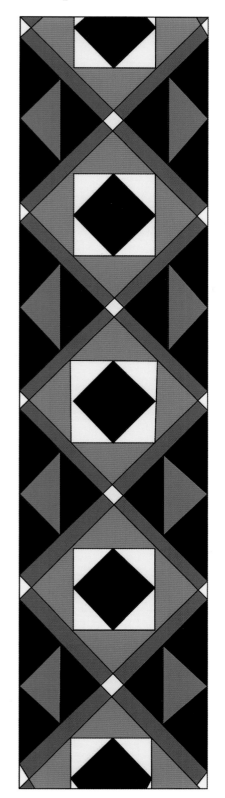

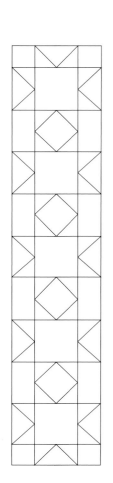

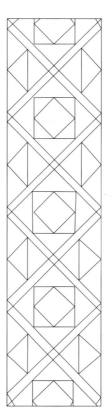

# Acknowledgments

I have many people to whom I owe my appreciation for their encouragement and support in writing this book:

- Neil Porter, for being a wonderful husband, an outstanding professional photographer and always on hand for 'just one more shot'.
- Sally Ablett who spent many hours stitching in-the-ditch, and hemming the bindings of many of the quilts, for quilting 'Mystic Sunflower' and giving general 'you can do it' encouragement.
- Rebecca Bolt of Husqvarna Viking Sewing Machines for introducing me to the Designer 2.
- Cheryl Brown of David & Charles for her quiet encouragement and belief in me, together with Sandra Pruski, Lisa Forrester, and proof reader and advisor Betsy Hosegood for their attention to detail and hard work.
- Beryl Cadman for completing the quilting of 'Purple Prose', 'Floral Tiled Floor' and 'Turning the Corner'.
- Barbara Chainey, Lynne Edwards, Dianne Huck and Joen Wolfrom for their sage advice and friendship.
- Rachel, Sheila and John of Creative Grids for their floor tiles and generous helpings of batting and rulers.
- Jackfield Tile Museum staff for their kindness and patience and allowing us access to the archives.
- Tracey Periera for quilting 'Let the Sun Shine'.
- Ann Rhodes for her graphic design skills.
- Jenny Spencer for quilting 'Stripey Hugs & Kisses', 'Turn of the Season' and giving the ideas for quilting 'Let the Sun Shine'.
- Maggie Rowell & Sharon Woods of Woodrow Studios for supplying fabric and friendship.
- Darra Williamson, my good friend from the United States, who encouraged me in this and other quilting ventures.
- Quilt shops of Great Britain and the United States for encouraging me to build up my collection of floor-tile fabrics.

## Bibliography

BELANGER GRAFTON Carol
*Decorative Tile Designs*
(Dover Publications Inc. 1992)
ISBN 0-486-26952-3

BRACKMAN Barbara
*Encyclopedia of Pieced Quilt Patterns*
(American Quilter's Society, 1993)
ISBN 0-89145-815-8

BRUYERE André
*Pavimenti – San Marco, Venezia*
*Instituto Poligrafico e Zecca Dello Stato*
ISBN 88-240-0467-9

MATHIESON Judy
*Mariner's Compass Quilts – New Directions*
(C&T Publications, 1995)
ISBN 0-914881-97-3

RILEY Noel
*Tile Art*
The Apple Press
ISBN 1-85076-107-8

SAMMARTINI Tudy
*Pavimenti a Venezia*
(Vianello Libri, 1999)
ISBN 88-7200-069-6

THOMPSON Shauna
*Distinctive Designs in Continuous Line*
(Powell Publications, 2000)
Powellpubl@aol.com

WALNER Hari
*Trapunto by Machine*
(C&T Publications, 1996)
ISBN 1-57120-006-1

## Useful Addresses

**All Saints Church, Bristol**
1, All Saints Court
Bristol BS1 1JN

**Bristol Cathedral**
Abbey Gatehouse, College Green
Bristol BS1 5TJ
www.bristol-cathedral.co.uk

**Creative Grids (UK) Ltd**
PO Box 207
Leicester LE3 6YP
www.creativegrids.com

**Husqvarna Viking Sewing Machines**
Viking House
Cheddar Business Park, Wedmore Road
Cheddar BS27 3EB
www.husqvarnaviking.com

**St Andrew's Cathedral, Inverness**
Ardross Street
Inverness IV3 5NS
www.inverness-cathedral.org.uk

**Jackfield Tile Museum**
Ironbridge Gorge Museums
Ironbridge
Shropshire TF8 7AW
Email: info@ironbridge.org.uk

**Holy Trinity Church, Kendal**
Kirkland
Kendal
Cumbria LA9 5AF
www.kendalparishchurch.co.uk

**Church of Saint Mary, Rydal**
Rydal Hill
Rydal
Cumbria LA22 9LX
www.rydalhall.org

**St Stephen's Church, Bristol**
St Stephen's Street
Bristol BS1 1EQ

# Index

Note: Page numbers in italics refer to illustrations